Christopher Cowie is an American who has been living in Florence for the past seven years. As a journalist in California he wrote on a variety of subjects including food and wine. He has become Italian in one way that was crucial to the making of this book: he now spends a far greater amount of time eating out, and on discussions of eating and drinking in general. These pursuits are Italian national pastimes. Recently he has written the text for a book of photographs by Béla Kalman entitled Ten Towns of Tuscany.

Acknowledgements

My thanks to the following people for their help in preparing this book.

Ramon Bejarano, Cinzia Cassai, Carla Cau, Carla Corsinovi, Roberta Cowie, Lucia Corti, Kelda Jones, Heidi and Roger Lascelles, Aduau Marshall, Benedetta and Fabio Picchi, Donatella Pirozzo and Pamela Scaramelli.

The cover illustration is a reproduction of an oil painting by the Florentine artist Romano Stefanelli, formerly a student of Pietro Annigoni. Signor Stefanelli's father, Giacomo, was a cook in some of the top Florentine trattorie. The artist's studio in Florence is at Via S. Egidio 12. Tel: 2480587

Maps reproduced from the Plan of Florence by kind permission of L.A.C., Florence as authorized Jun 12/90

EATING OUT IN FLORENCE

Christopher Cowie

Tower Press Florence

Via Madonna della Pace 62

50125 - Firenze

Publication Data

Title Eating out in Florence
Drawings Aduau Marshall
Printing Karta, Firenze

Copyright© Christopher Cowie

Distribution
Beyond Italy:
Africa, South Africa - Faradawn
Americas, Canada - International Travel Maps
Australasia - Australia Rex Publications

Roger Lascelles, Brentford (Middx):
Belgium, Germany, GB/ Ireland, Netherlands,
Switzerland, Scandinavia, Denmark, Finland, Norway
Sweden, New Zealand

Contents

Forward
Introduction to Tuscan Food
Florence - An Outline Plan

PART 1
Our Zones of Florence- (Clockwise starting south of the railway station)

1 Ognissanti	17
2 Santa Maria Novella	31
3 The Duomo	45
4 Santa Croce	55
5 Piazza Signoria	75
6 Ponte Vecchio	89
7 Santa Trinita	101
8 Santo Spirito	117
9 Outside Florence	131
10 A Selection of Tuscan Restaurants	146

PART 2

1 The Wines of Tuscany	151
2 A Selection of Tuscan Wine Producers	166
3 Selected Recipes	180
4 Glossary	201
5 Index	209

Forward

"Could you please direct us to a good trattoria nearby?" you ask, giving it all the charm you've got. For most travelers this is no idle query. No matter what artistic glories you may have witnessed, or traveler's indignities you may have suffered, the overall tally of the day's success hangs not a little on where you end up for lunch and dinner.

This book is designed to give the visitor an overview of what's on offer in Florence. We also hope that *Eating Out in Florence* will find a place on your shelves as a source book for Tuscan foods, wines and recipes.

Since Florence must entertain more than one million visitors a year, many of its eating places cater directly to tourists. We have not given any space to tourist traps, not even to warn you off them. The telltale signs are only too obvious, (e.g., menus in four languages and busloads of tourists milling about).

In any case, the dozens of places we've recommended should keep you out of harm's way. Don't be put off, however, to find fellow travelers dining alongside you at that special authentic place we've sent you to. Florence is small, so almost all the best restaurants and trattorie in town bring in their share of foreign visitors.

We have divided Florence into neighborhoods, or *quartieri*, most of them named after churches, in the Florentine manner.

Buon Appetito and Salute.

INTRODUCTION TO TUSCAN FOOD

The undisputed star of Tuscan cooking is nature herself. Regional dishes owe everything to the high quality of the fruits, vegetables and herbs, olives and grapes, meat, game and poultry which thrive on the rich Tuscan soil. The famous Tuscan character - pragmatic, critical, tolerant only of things authentic - expresses itself best in its insistence on not spoiling the gifts that nature has provided. What can hardly be overstated is the deep quasi-mystical attachment Tuscans have for the land.

The fundamentals of Tuscan cooking are quickly summed up: take the best ingredients available at their freshest and prepare them simply, with consummate respect for the essential nature of each food. In other words, give the imagination a holiday, hold the frills, don't go tampering with a good thing!

What allows this rigorous, tradition-bound approach to shine is the presence of one of the greatest gastronomic gifts of all: Tuscan olive oil. Generally regarded by gourmets the world over as the supreme oil for the kitchen (challenged only by oil from Provence) Tuscan olive oil is the condiment for all seasons, enlivening dishes with its fruity, peppery flavour. You can judge a restaurant's ambitions instantly by the quality of the olive oil found on its tables. Immediately after pressing, most Tuscan oils are a dusky emerald green until the sediment settles after a few months. Some fine oils in the southern part of the region are golden hued. Of course the quality of olive oil, like wine, varies according to the terrain and the producer. At the top level, olive oil production has become about as sophisticated as modern winemaking.

Historically, the other Tuscan staple has always been the most basic foodstuff of all: bread. In many Florentine restaurants you will find hearty farmer dishes thickened with bread. Ribollita is a vegetable soup with black cabbage and bread, Pappa al Pomodoro is a soup of tomato, basil and garlic with bread, and Panzanella is a cold summer salad of cucumber, onions, basil and bread.

One peculiarity of Tuscan bread is that it contains no salt. This dates back to the days when salt was a luxury and the

Tuscans decided they could do without. Most Tuscans today swear by their saltless bread. But then, they remedy the deficiency by salting everything else.

In Tuscany meat and poultry are usually grilled, fried, or roasted and served with nothing but a wedge of lemon. Vegetables are cooked simply, often with garlic, and always with olive oil. Raw vegetables are dipped in olive oil, salt and pepper.

A delicious starter, or antipasto, called Fettunta is no - thing but a slice of toasted bread rubbed with raw garlic, sprinkled with salt and doused with olive oil.

While simplicity is the key, there are certain dishes once cooked by country grandmothers which require long hours of loving attention before being brought to perfection. There is nothing particularly complicated or fancy about these dishes, but they do require various stages of preparation and hence, lots of patience. These dishes, which largely disappeared from Tuscan tables with the onslaught of hurried modern life, are making a comeback in some of the most celebrated restaurants in Florence which specialize in re-creating the old recipes of careful country cooking.

(i.e. Cibreo, La Baraonda, Osteria 1, La Carabaccia, and La Rucola among others).

THE TUSCAN MENU

Antipasti-Starters

Crostini:
>toasted bread topped with various spreads, usually of chicken livers, capers, anchovies. Others include black olive paste, porcini mushrooms, pesto, chopped tomatoes and cheese.

Fettunta:
>toasted bread rubbed with raw garlic and dipped in olive oil

Salumi:
>mixed cold cuts; can be salami, prosciutto, mortadella (the original bologna), finocchiona (a fennel flavored salami).

Primi - First courses

Acquacotta:
>light vegetable and mushroom soup served with toasted bread and a poached egg

Cacciucco:
>fish stew with tomatoes, chili peppers, and red wine

Carabaccia:
>thick onion soup

Minestra di farro:
>emmer and bean soup

Panzanella:
>cold salad of tomatoes, cucumber, onions, basil, bread and olive oil

Pappa al pomodoro:
>thick bread soup with tomatoes and basil

Pappardelle alla lepre:
>egg pasta with wild rabbit sauce

Penne strascicate:
>macaroni "dragged through" a ragú sauce

Ravioli:
> ravioli filled with spinach and ricotta

Ribollita:
> vegetable soup thickened with bread

Risotto nero:
> rice cooked with cuttlefish squid and its black ink

Tortelli:
> potato filled ravioli pouches

Zuppa di fagioli:
> bean soup

Secondi - Main courses

Arista:
> roast pork loin with rosemary and garlic

Baccalà alla Livornese:
> salt cod cooked with tomatoes and garlic

Bistecca alla fiorentina:
> T-bone steak charcoal grilled

Fritto misto:
> fried meats and vegetables (chicken, rabbit, lamb; zucchini, zucchini flowers, artichokes, mushrooms)

Lombatina:
> grilled veal chop

Peposo:
> peppery beef stew

Pollo alla diavola (or *la mattone*):
> brick-flattened, grilled chicken

Spiedini di maiale:
> pork loin on a skewer

Stracotto:
> long cooked beef with tomatoes and red wine

Totani all'inzimino:
> squid with beet greens or spinach and tomatoes

Trippa alla fiorentina:
    tripe with tomatoes and parmesan cheese

Contorni - vegetable/salad side dishes

Fagioli all'olio:
    white beans with olive oil

Fagioli all'uccelletto:
    white beans in sauce of tomatoes, garlic and sage

Spinaci saltati:
    spinach sautéed in garlic and oil

Pinzimonio:
    raw vegetables dipped in olive oil, salt and pepper

Fiori fritti:
    fried zucchini flowers

Dolci- desserts

Cantuccini di Prato:
    hard almond cookies (served with Vin Santo)

Castagnaccio:
    bland cake made with chestnut four, raisins, walnuts and pine nuts

Torta della Nonna:
    Pie filled with pastry cream, topped with powdered sugar

Panforte:
    hard, spiced fruit and nut cake from medieval Siena

Schiacciata alla Fiorentina:
    saffron colored cake topped with powdered sugar (made during Carnival period)

Schiacciata con l'uva:
    flatbread covered with dark wine grapes (and plenty of seeds) and sugar, made during grape harvest in autumn

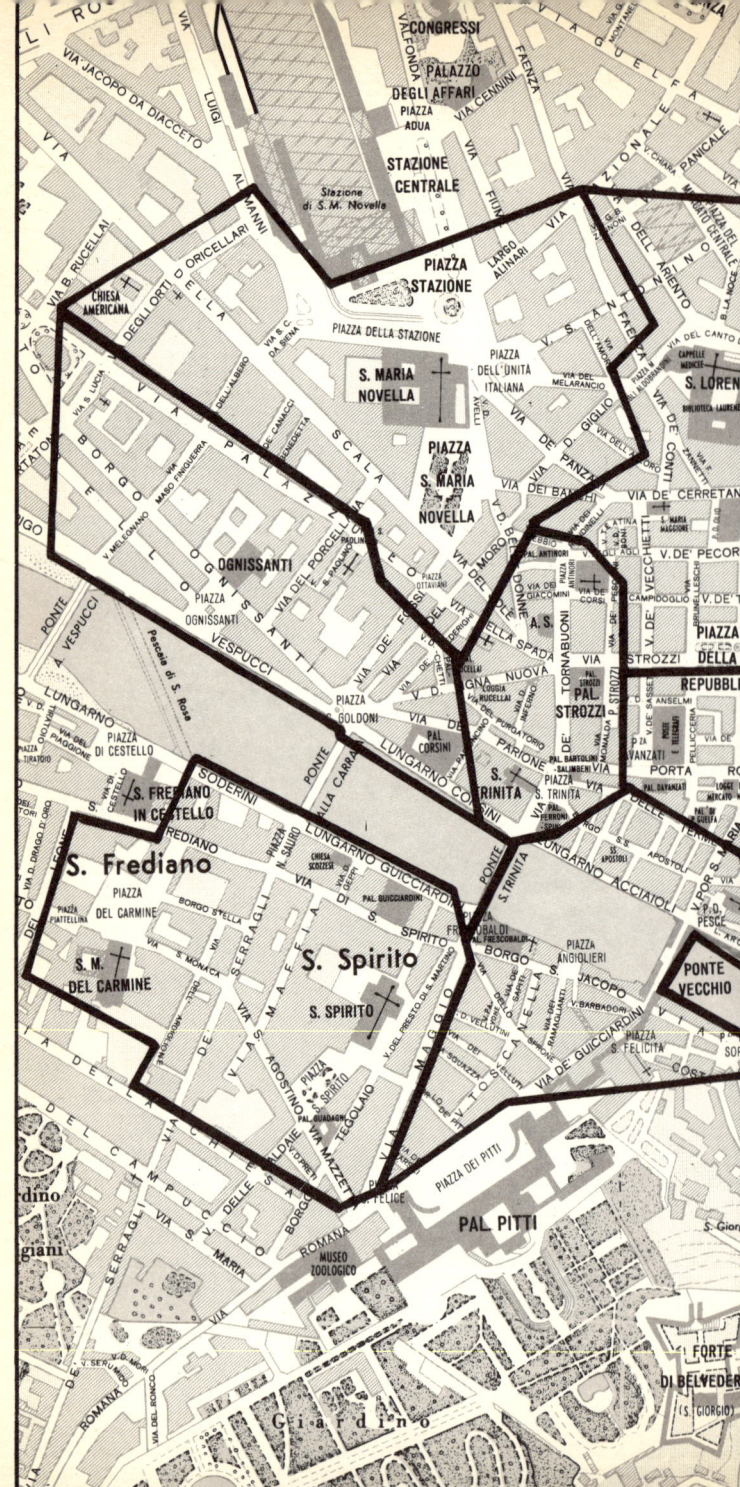

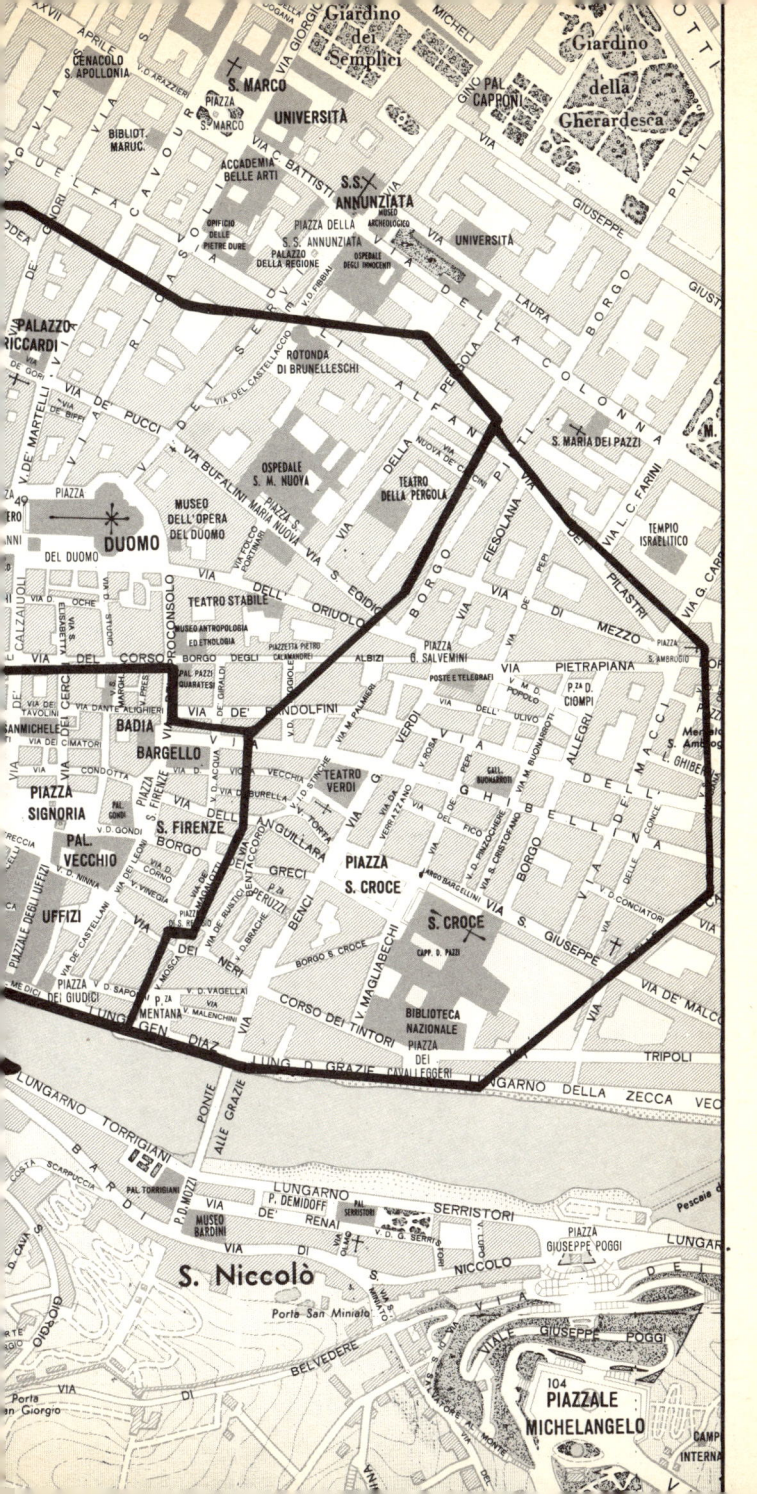

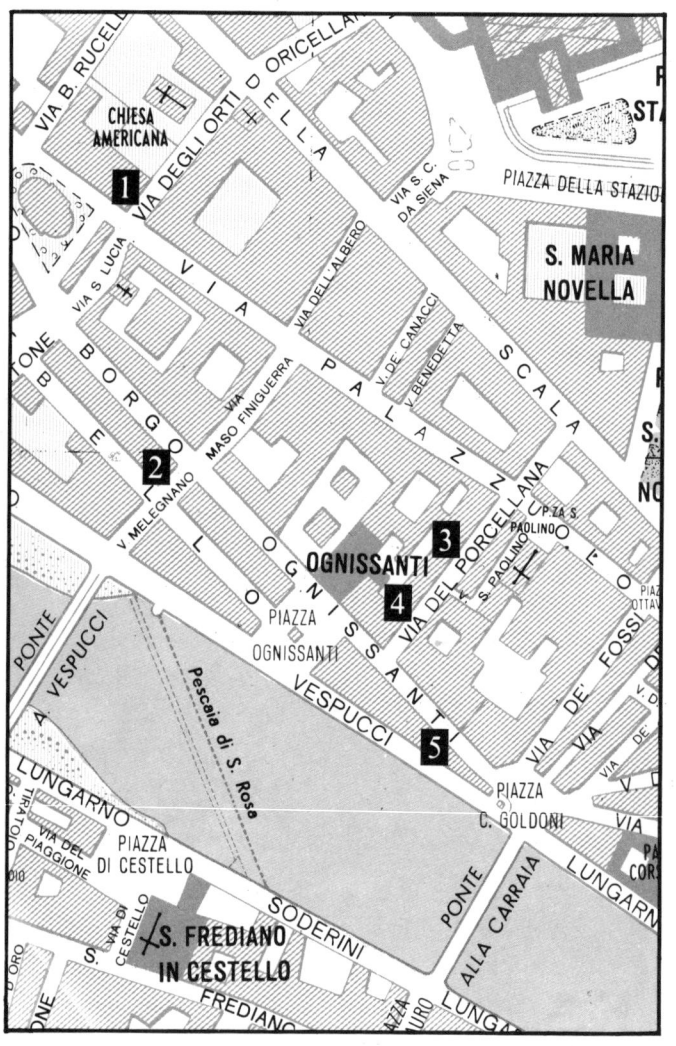

OGNISSANTI

The beautiful church of Ognissanti was founded in 1256 by a Benedictine order expert in the manufacturing of wool. The area of Ognissanti became the center of the Florentine wool industry which was the basis of the city's medieval economy. The church was rebuilt in the Gothic style during the 17th century.

1. La Carabaccia

2. Il Profeta

3. Sostanza

4. 13 Gobbi

5. Harry's Bar

La Carabaccia

Via Palazzuolo 190
Tel. 214782
Closed: Sun
Credit Cards: Visa, Eurocard, MC
Reservations: Advisable
Price: High moderate

TUSCAN INVENTIONS WITH HERBS

This fine restaurant bases its fare on traditional Tuscan cuisine, but also likes to explore variations on themes. Fragrant products of the Tuscan countryside like nipitella (a minty wild herb), wild asparagus, bay leaf, leeks, juniper and rughetta perform wonderful feats in flavoring the meat and fish dishes of La Carabaccia. No matter how innovative, these dishes could never have been invented anywhere but in the heart of Tuscany. *Sformati*, best described as crustless quiches, or perhaps soufflés not meant to rise, are a specialty here, made from all sorts of vegetables and legumes.

La Carabaccia is the name for Tuscan Onion soup. Gastronomic history comes to life with the debate over this dish. According to Tuscans, Catherine de' Medici took the recipe, along with her convoy of chefs, to Paris in 1533 when she became the bride of the future Henry II. Naturally, the acute Parisians seized on the recipe, to the extent that today a bowl of soup a l'oignon is practically a national symbol of France.

La Carabaccia starts you off with freebies of black olives and bits of buttered garlic toast. The decor is simple and pleasant, with ceramics and copper pots and a smattering of plants.

Antipasti

AFFETTATI TOSCANI
Prosciutto, salame, paté

Primi

ZUPPA CARABACCIA
Tuscan onion soup
MALFATTI DI BIETOLA
Vegetable ravioli filling without the pasta
SFOGLIATA AL PESTO
Pastry with pesto
RISOTTO ZUCCHE E FIORI
Risotto of zucchini and zucchini flowers

Secondi

ARISTA ALLA MELUVA
Roast pork with grapes and apples
SFORMATO DI PORRI
Crustless quiche of leeks (or seasonal legumes)

Dolci

TRIS DELLA CASA
Tastes of three:
Soft cheeses whipped and scented with lemon or raspberry
Chocolate mousse
Raspberry or chocolate cake

IL PROFETA

Borgo Ognissanti 93/r
Tel. 212265
Closed: Sun/Mon & three weeks in August
Credit Cards: Visa, Amex
Reservations: Advisable
Price: High moderate

THE PROPHET DELIVERS

An attractive restaurant with a fine wooden ceiling and well-laid tables whose linen depicts Florentine monuments. The walls are covered with paintings of Tuscan landscapes. The clientele, in this area full of hotels, is a mix of tourists and locals. The service is professional and courteous.

The cuisine is mostly Tuscan. An excellent dish here is the Panzerotti all'Abruzzese, rich and creamy, straight from the oven.

Fish is also handled well, as demonstrated by the fresh salmon in a sauce with capers. The tossed salad is made from seasonal field greens.

Antipasti

CARPACCIO DI STAGIONE
Thin sliced raw beef
ANTIPASTI TOSCANA
Sliced prosciutto, salami, etc.

Primi

PENNETTE DEL PROFETA
Penne with bacon, mushrooms, tomato and cream
PANZEROTTI ALL'ABRUZZESE
Crepes with prosciutto, mozzarella cheese and bechamel
TAGLIOLINI "FRESCHI" AL POMODORO
E BASILICO
Homemade tagliolini with tomato and basil

Secondi

SCALOPPINE DI VITELLA ALLA CAMPAGNOLA
Veal scaloppine with tomato, mushroom, and basil
PETTO DI POLLO ALLA BASCHESE
Breast of chicken with bell peppers
TRANCIA DI SALMONE ALLA GRENOBLESE
Salmon steak with sauce of capers

Dolci

ZUPPA DEL "PROFETA"
Zabaione with mascarpone cheese
CREM CARAMEL
Caramel custard
FRAGOLE A PIACERE
Strawberries (in season)

Sostanza (Il Troia)

Via Porcellana 25/r
Tel. 212691
Closed: Sat/Sun
Credit Cards: No
Reservations: Not necessary
Price: High moderate

A FLORENTINE LANDMARK

Sostanza is a small neighborhood trattoria that has been around since 1869. A visit here is part of many tours of the intimate Florence. Though Sostanza is still invariably described as a 'working man's' trattoria, which I take to mean a place for men who perform some sort of labor, the clientele is by now distinctly gentrified.

Sostanza has maintained its long comunal tables - first come, first served - and its plain decor and cutlery. The food is strictly Tuscan. Sostanza is particularly known for its fried chicken breasts which come swimming in butter (better to transfer the delicious chicken out of the pan and onto your plate. To eat it out of all that butter, as some people do, must be ruinously rich to the system). And of course there's the Bistecca Fiorentina, grilled briefly, to perfection.

Some neighborhood regulars have been eating at Sostanza for half a century. Famous guests to have eaten here include Chagall, Steinbeck, Pound, and actors Peck, Steiger and Reagan. Among the many celebrated Italians to have frequented Sostanza are the artists Annigoni and Guarnieri.

Antipasti

MISTO TOSCANO
Crostini and cured meats

Primi

ZUPPA PAESANA
Soup of bread, cabbage and other vegetables
MINESTRE PASTA E FAGIOLI
Bean and macaroni soup
TORTELLINI FRESCHI
Fresh homemade tortellini pasta

Secondi

PETTO DI POLLO AL BURRO
Chicken breast fried in butter
AGNELLO IN UMIDO
Stewed lamb with tomatoes
BISTECCA ALLA FIORENTINA
Florentine beefsteak

Dolci

TORTA DELLA NONNA
Cream pie
PANNA COTTA
Rich cooked cream

13 GOBBI' (13 DWARVES)

Via Porcellana 9
Tel: 298769
Closed: Sun/Mon
Credit Card: Visa, MC, Diners
Reservations: Advisable
Price: High Moderate

13 HUNGARIAN DWARVES

This restaurant is something of a curiosity. It was opened years ago by a Hungarian soccer player who had come to Florence to play for La Fiorentina, the local professional team.

The name means the '13 Dwarves', perhaps referring to the fact that the Ognissanti area was historically the ghetto to which ill and deformed people were ostracized. The menu once specialized in Hungarian dishes and still today offers Hungarian goulash. The tables in the central room are equipped with circular 'booths', as we Americans say. Together with the soft lighting and all the wood in the decor, they create an atmosphere of intimacy and romance. Two other dining rooms have a charm of their own, the walls crowded with paintings and memorabilia.

The cuisine is Tuscan and classic Italian and enjoys a faithful following by locals who have obviously come to appreciate the combination of good food and a setting about as romantic as unsentimental Florence ever gets.

Antipasti

CARPACCIO DI PESCE SPADA AFFUMICATO
Slices of smoked raw swordfish
FAGIOLI E GAMBERETTI O RUCOLA E GAMBE-
RETTI
Shrimp with white beans or rucola lettuce

Primi

MACCHERONCETTI STRASCICATI
Macaroni with ragu
RAVIOLI DELLA CASA AL GORGONZOLA O ROSE'
Homemade ravioli with gorgonzola or rosè sauce

Secondi

COSTOLA DI VITELLA CON CARCIOFI
Veal rib with artichokes
SCALOPPA ALLA "13 GOBBI"
Fried veal scaloppine with tomato and mozzarella
SALMONE FRESCO ALLA GRIGLIA
O AL BURRO E SALVIA
Fresh salmon, grilled, or cooked in butter and sage
SOGLIOLA DEL TIRRENO ALLA GRIGLIA
O ALLA MUGNAIA
Fresh sole, grilled or sauteed in butter

Dolci

CANTUCCI DI PRATO CON VIN SANTO
Hard almond cookies with sweet wine
DOLCI A SCELTA AL CARRELLO
Selections from the sweet trolley

Harry's Bar

Lungarno Vespucci 22
Tel: 296700 (will take 2396700)
Closed: Sun
Credit Cards: Visa, Amex
Reservations: Advisable (for dinner)
Price: Expensive

WHAT'S IN A NAME?

At Harry's the dollar is always strong (come on, let's make believe!) and the American is always a guest of honor. Here the experience of being an American in Europe, with all its ups and downs, is rounded into a distinct sense of well-being as we settle into our beloved cocktail hour. Not that Harry's caters only to Americans; the clubby atmosphere here embraces all nationalities.

What's in a name? Whatever's been put into that name over the years. In this case, we're talking about decades of entertaining those foreign travelers, as well as locals, who want a taste of the style that is Harry's alone.

Your host and barman, Leo Vadorini, presides over cocktail hour with a crisp energy that suggests something big is always about to happen, that Harry himself is going to show up, or at least some American movie-star of a bygone era. And to dine well you don't have to move. Simply stay on at Harry's. Be sure to check that there's a table available, however.

We're always grateful for the buzz we get at Harry's and for the excellent Bellinis (peach nectar and spumante). For the die-hard Martini drinker, Harry's are the best in town.

Antipasti

PROSCIUTTO DI VITELLA AFFUMICATO
Smoked veal prosciutto
COCKTAIL DI GAMBERETTI
Shrimp cocktail

Primi

TAGLIERINI AL FORNO GRATINATI
Taglierini with chopped ham, oven-crisped
CANNELLONI
Cannelloni of veal, spinach and nutmeg

Secondi

SCAMPI A LA "HARRY"
Shrimp with rice pilaf and cream sauce
CLUB SEGRETO
Club sandwich with fresh chicken
PETTO DI POLLO AL CURRY CON RISO
Breast of chicken with curry and rice pilaf

Dolci

TORTA ALLE MELE
Apple pie
CREPES AL GRAND MARNIER

Baccus
Borgo Ognissanti 45/r
Tel: 283714
Closed: Sun

Every day of the week, Baccus offers a different menu which includes two-dozen pasta variations. This restaurant offers quick, inexpensive pastas at lunchtime, catering to the office crowd, however the dishes do suffer from being served cafeteria-style.

Fortunately, in the evening Baccus gives pasta the care it deserves and produces some splendid results.

Baldini
Via Panzani 57/red
Tel. 283331
Closed: Sat

Near the Teatro Comunale, popular with the musicians.

Il Gourmet
Via Il Prato 68/r
Tel. 214424
Closed: Sun

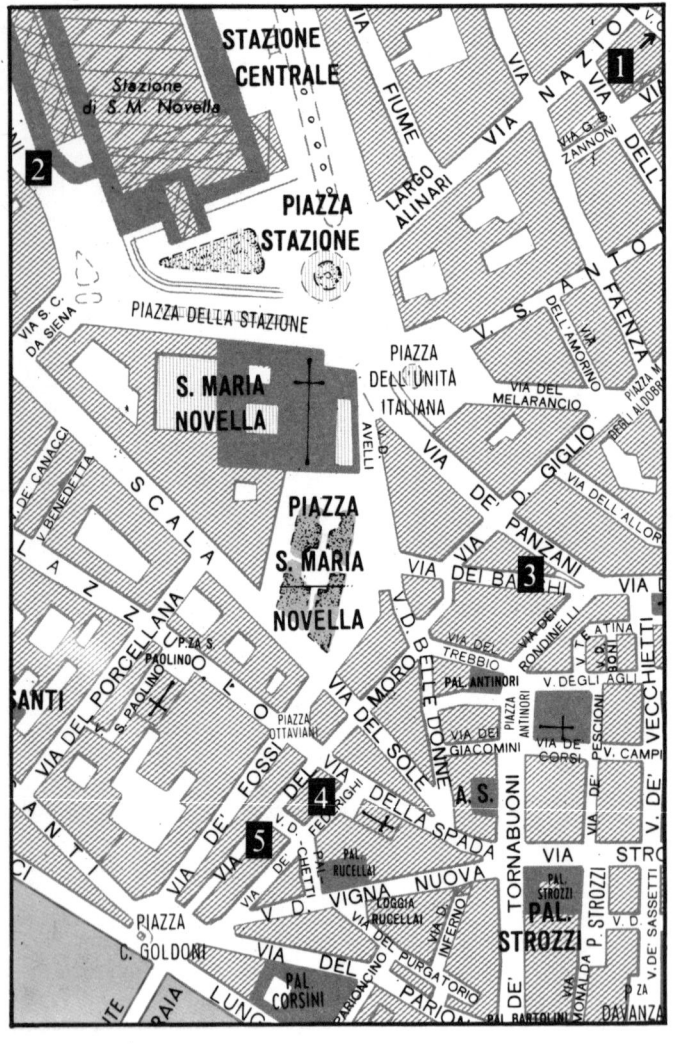

SANTA MARIA NOVELLA

Medieval church built by the Domenican order. The upper half of the splendid facade was designed later by one of the most versatile of all Renaissance men, Leon Battista Alberti, architect, painter, sculptor, poet, musician, soldier, etc.

1. La Taverna Di Bronzino

2. Otello

3. Sabatini

4. Trattoria Garga

5. Osteria Numero Uno

TAVERNA DEL BRONZINO

Via delle Ruote 25/red
Tel. 495220
Closed: Sun
Credit cards: All
Reservations: Necessary
Price: Expensive

ALL AROUND EXCELLENCE

(The Taverna does not actually fall within our SMN zone but we have included it here anyway because it is just a short walk from the center and well worth visiting).

The sober fifteenth century palazzo which houses the Taverna has connections with the Florentine painter Bronzino, hence the name. The Taverna has been open for seven years and is one of Florence's most talked about restaurants. Here all aspects of the business are looked after with fastidious care. The service is attentive and friendly without a hint of pretension. Almost palpable is the satisfaction that the men at the Taverna take in guiding guests through excellent meals accompanied by superb wines. The Florentine press talks about the Taverna in terms of the friendships which thrive here.

So where does the Taverna stand on the raging questions of regional versus national cooking, nouvelle cuisine vis-a-vis traditional fare? Somewhere in the uncontentious middleground, where respect for tradition co-exists happily with the need for creativity.

As an example, there's the fresh grilled salmon with ginger sauce. The homemade pastas often come with unusual and scrumptious sauces. The trolley of roast meats is, however, the usual classic centerpiece of the evening menu. If there isn't something special you want from the wine list, let the waiters guide you. They know what they're doing.

Antipasti

BURRATA (Crostini)
Toasted bread slices with:
Butter and mozzarella, salmon and swordfish, porcini mushrooms

Primi

TORTELLONI AL CEDRO
Large stuffed pasta with sauce of citrus peels and cream
RIGATONCINI CON SALSA RUSTICA
Rigatoni pasta with sausage, red chicory and hot pepper sauce
RAVIOLI ALL'ERBA CIPOLLINA
Ravioli with chives

Secondi

GRAN PEZZO AL PEPE VERDE
Standing rib roast with hot peppers
CARRELLO DI ARROSTI
Trolley of roasted meats
Beef fillet, Beef Wellington, leg of lamb, roast beef
UCCELLETTO DI VITELLO AGLI ASPARAGI
Pieces of veal scaloppine with asparagus
CARTONCINI DI VITELLA AI CARCIOFI
Veal and artichoke baked in foil paper

Dolci

PANNA COTTA CON LAMPONI
Rich cooked cream with raspberries
BAVARESE AL CIOCCOLATO
Cream pudding with chocolate

OTELLO

a Orti Oricellari 36/red
Tel. 215819
Closed: Tue
Credit card: All
Reservations: Advisable
Price: High moderate

TRADITIONAL MENU AND UNIQUE TASTING SESSION

Just a few steps from track #1 at the train station, Otello often goes unnoticed by visitors anxious to get into the heart of the city. A blessing for anyone who would like to eat well without straying far from the trains, this tasteful, air conditioned restaurant is a good bet regardless of your travel plans.

Although countless touches put us in mind of a classical Italian restaurant (the nattily dressed waiters, the ice buckets for spumante, the fresh cherries plunged into ice-water at your table, and the variety of fish dishes on the menù), Otello was founded over 40 years ago for the purpose of offering humble dishes from the Tuscan countryside.

Otello kept the faith even when many country dishes, like the thick bread-based soups Ribollita and Pappa al Pomodoro, went out of fashion in the 1970's. A look at the size of those Florentine steaks displayed in the entrance ought to convince you that Otello is out to give you the real Tuscan experience. Even so, by now a great many classical dishes have crept onto the menu and Otello should be categorized as a hybrid restaurant.

A brilliant innovation at Otello is the chance to taste small portions of a series of Tuscan dishes, each accompanied by a different fine Tuscan wine. This menu is offered at a fixed price, wines included, which is very reasonable. With all the interest in the new Tuscan wines on the market, this an idea destined to spread. Ask for the *degustazione* menu.

Antipasti

INSALATA DI OVULI E PARMIGIANO
Salad of mushrooms and parmesan
CARPACCIO DI MANZO
Thin sliced seasoned raw beef

Primi

PAPPARDELLE AL CAPRIOLO
Noodles with roe-deer
GNOCCHETTI GORGONZOLA E SPINACI
Little gnocchi with gorgonzola and spinach

Secondi

OSSOBUCO ALLA FIORENTINA
Veal on the bone in tomatoe sauce
BISTECCA ALLA FIORENTINA
Florentine beefsteak
BRANZINO AL CARTOCCIO
Sea Bass baked in foil paper
MISTO DI PESCE ALLA GRIGLIA
Mix grilled fish

Dolci

DOLCI AL CARRELLO
Trolley of cake and puddings
MACEDONIA
Fruit salad

SABATINI

Via Panzani 41/43
Tel. 211559
Closed: Mon (open all summer)
Credit Card: Yes
Reservations: Advisable
Price: Expensive

YESTERYEAR'S CHAMPION IS STILL GOING STRONG

On one point all Florentines will invariably agree: Sabatini was once the best restaurant in town. Not only that, it was considered, in the words of a local gastronome, "the very platonic ideal of a restaurant" which presumably means that Plato himself couldn't have imagined anything finer. In the 1950's and 60's Sabatini had an enormous reputation, especially in New York City. VIPs, local and international, flocked to this citadel of fashionable dining.

The poorly informed may go on to say, "But it's not what it used to be", making of Sabatini the whipping boy for all the good things Florentine which haven't survived into modern times.

Well, the truth is that there is little need to pine for the past over this restaurant. Sabatini today is in excellent hands. The team of five professionals that took over in 1979 has maintained the traditional atmosphere and high standards. Sabatini remains super chic, with service in the grand style, and its traditional clientele is back. The food can be memorable. I'm thinking of the delicate white sauce on the porcini mushroom starter, the excellent marinated fish, the rich and creamy crespelle, the tender herb-flavored leg of lamb, and the pear cooked in red wine.

An indoor garden pours light into what would otherwise be a dark space given the wood-paneled walls. The restaurant is air-conditioned and includes an American bar. Fine wines are available, naturally.

Antipasti

ANTIPASTI ALLA SABATINI
Marinated fish
INSALATA DI FUNGHI PORCINI
Porcini mushroom salad

Primi

PANZEROTTI
Crepes with ham and cheese in bechamel sauce,
oven-crisped
MACCHERONCETTI ALLA NORMA
Macaroni with eggplant, tomato and basil
RISOTTO CON PUNTE DI ASPARAGI
Risotti with asparagus tips

Secondi

SCAMPI ALLA PESCATORE
Prawns in white wine, tomato and garlic
COSCIOTTO DI AGNELLO AL FORNO
Roasted milk lamb with fresh herbs
COSTOLETTA DI VITELLA DELLO CHEF
Veal ribs with eggplant and mozzarella

Dolci

ZUCCOTTINO CON CIOCCOLATO CALDO
Chilled cake and ice cream with hot chocolate

Trattoria Garga

Via del Moro 48/red
Tel.: 2398898
Closed: Mon. Open only evenings.
Credit Cards: Amex
Reservations: Recommended
Price: Expensive

A SPECIAL EVENING SPOT

Garga is one of the most delightful eating establishments in Florence. You need only peek through its windows to be charmed. Inside amid colorful frescoed walls, statues, plants and inviting place settings, we imagine we could be happy with little difficulty- especially if the food measures up. Well, it does, and then some.

Chef Giuliano Garga, aided by his Canadian wife Sharon, has come up with some interesting inventions to complement the standard Tuscan repertoire. The fresh pastas come with unusual sauces, like that of Taglierini del Magnifico named after Lorenzo de Medici who was famous for throwing sumptuous banquets. The salads of field greens are put together with flair.

Meat and fish dishes are excellent, including an impressive lamb dish with a spicy rosè sauce and the scampi prawns. For dessert, we strongly recommend Sharon's unbeatable cheesecake. Garga's wine list is brief owing to the lack of cellar space. But the bottles on hand - mostly Tuscan wines - are of a high quality.

Evenings at Garga tend to go on and on since guests are reluctant to leave the lovely surroundings. Giuliano and Sharon have therefore decided to concentrate on the evenings, staying open late to satisfy demand, but no longer opening for lunch. That's bad news for the lunch crowd.

Antipasti

INSALATA DEL GARGA
Avocado, escarole, tomato, pine nuts, parmesan
INSALATA DI ZUCCHINE
Grated zucchini and truffle oil

Primi

PENNETTE AL GORGONZOLA E ZUCCHINE
Macaroni with gorgonzola and zucchini
TAGLIATELLE ALLA VIGLIACCA
Tagliatelle with tomato, garlic, and chili pepper
TAGLIERINI DEL MAGNIFICO
Taglierini with citrus rinds, cream, parmesan, cognac

Secondi

FILETTINI DI VITELLA ALLA CHANTAL
Veal with asparagus and mustard sauce
AGNELLO ALLE BACCHE ROSA
Lamb with creamy, red pepper sauce.

Dolci

TORTA AL CIOCCOLATO
Chocolate cake
FRAGOLE CON ZABAIONE CHANTILLY
Strawberries with zabaione
TORTA DI MELE CON PANNA E PINOLI
Apple cake with cream and pine nuts
CHEESECAKE

OSTERIA NUMERO UNO

Via del Moro 18-20
Tel. 284897
Closed: Sunday August
Credit cards: Visa, MC, Diners
Reservations: Advisable
Price: Expensive

AN ELEGANT INN

The Osteria of Gianni Girardi, who got his training at Sabatini during its heyday, started life in a rustic cellar at Borgo Ognissanti Numero Uno. For years the chef was the celebrated Masino, who had cooked for illustrious Florentine families. When the gifted old man finally retired Sig. Girardi decided to offer a partnership to the best chef he could find. Aldo Magnago, who accepted that offer, happens to be from the north - bringing with him a knowing touch with risotto dishes - but had cooked in Florence long enough to have totally assimilated the Tuscan ways.

The Osteria's new home is soberly elegant with some beautiful pieces of furniture, a fireplace typical of Florentine palazzi but rarely seen in restaurants, and some wonderful old picture frames which seem candidates for the Uffizi gallery - even if the paintings within them fall inevitably short of the mark.

Showstoppers on the menu include the Ossobuco with porcini mushrooms, porcini mushrooms grilled on their own as a main course, and a delicate roast beef called Tagliata di Lorenzo de Medici. There are plenty of top wines to choose from as well as the excellent house wine, a Chianti by La Sala in nearby San Casciano.

Antipasti

SALAME TOSCANO CON FICHI
Tuscan salame with figs
PANZANELLA ALLA CAMPAGNOLA
Country bread salad
SALMONE AFFUMICATO DI SCOZIA
Scottish smoked salmon with toast

Primi

SFOGLIATINE DI RICOTTA E BASILICO
Pasta pouches filled with ricotta and fresh basil
TAGLIATELLE NERE CON SEPPIOLINE
Tagliatelle pasta with black-ink squid
TORTELLONI DI NASELLO
Tortelloni pasta stuffed with cod
FARFALLINE ALLE NOCI (see Recipes)
Butterfly pasta with walnut and sausage sauce

Secondi

SCAMPI GIGANTI ALLA GRIGLIA
Giant prawns grilled
TAGLIATA DI LORENZO DE MEDICI
Roast beef on the bone
FUNGHI PORCINI ALLA PARMIGIANA
Porcini mushrooms with tomato and parmesan cheese
FUNGHI PORCINI ALLA GRIGLIA
Porcini mushrooms grilled

Dolci

TORTA DELLA NONNA
Cream pie
MERINGATO ALLA FIORENTINA
Meringue

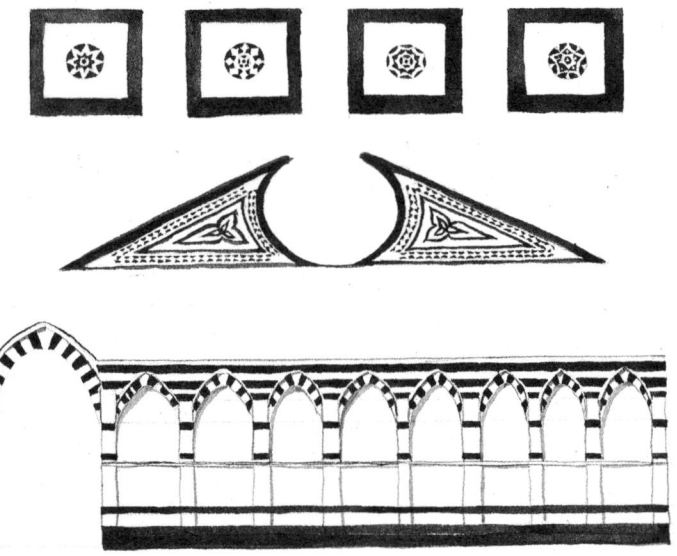

BUCA MARIO
Piazza degli Ottaviani 16/r
Tel. 214179
Closed: Wed and Thu lunch

PINOCCHIO
Via della Scala 28
Tel: 218418
Closed: Sat/Sun

IL COCCODRILLO
Via della Scala 5
Tel. 282600
Closed: Sun

CROCE AL TREBBIO
Via delle Belle Donne 49/r
Tel. 287089
Closed: Mon

IL SASSO DI DANTE
Piazza delle Pallottole 6/r
Tel. 28 2113
Closed: Thurs/Fri

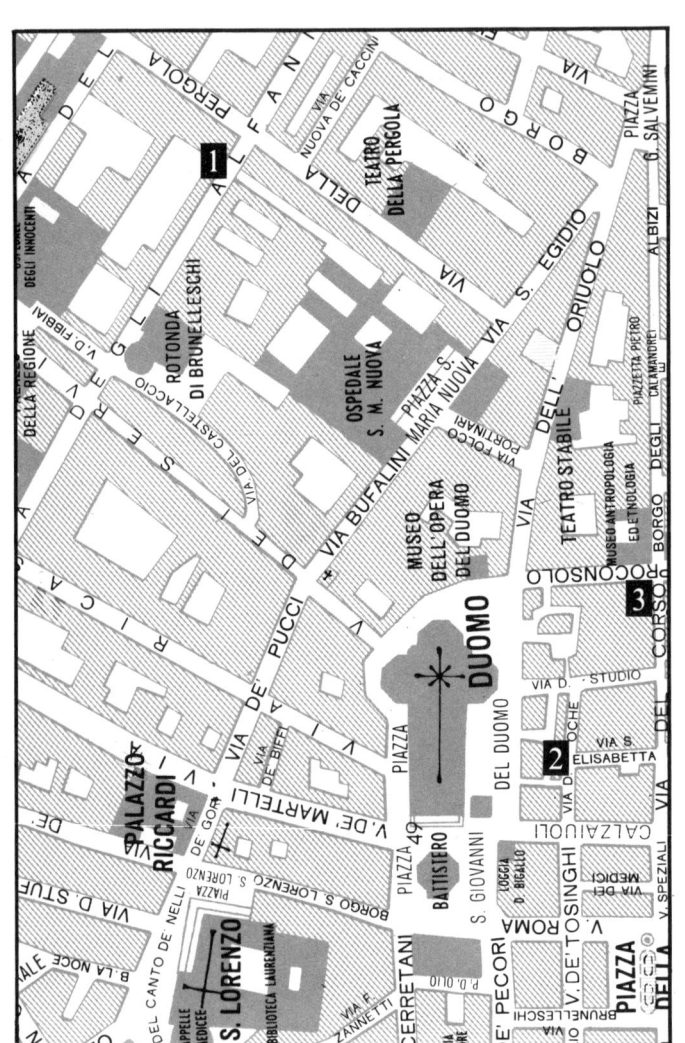

DUOMO

A Florentine saying is, "If you live within sight of the Dome, you will have good luck". Brunelleschi's engineering masterpiece is one of the largest domes in the world.

1. Gauguin

2. Ottorino

3. Mossacce

GAUGUIN

Via degli Alfani 24/red
Tel: 2340616
Closed: Sun/Mon lunch
Credit Cards: Amex, Visa
Reservations: Advisable
Price: Moderate

A FRENCHMAN CREATES

Jean-Michel Carasso didn't set out to create a vegetarian restaurant. He simply lost interest in meat for a variety of reasons including the fact that most menus in Florence are dominated by meat dishes. "So I cook everything else that isn't meat", he explains.

Jean-Michel is a Frenchmen who has lived in Florence for many years. He is a self-taught cook whose menu shows three distinct influences: French, Italian and Middle Eastern. Fish plays a large role in all courses.

Two small rooms in shades of blue show a distinct bias for things done with artistic flair. The tables contain little suprises. The menus are framed and hang above the tables. There is a whiff of Paris here. The light, healthy, creative dishes are just what a good many Florentines have been waiting for. Just a short walk from the Duomo, Gauguin could be a nice way for travelers to take a break from strictly regional fare.

The wine list is short but interesting and the beer is from a small Bavarian brewery.

Antipasti

INSALATA TIEPIDA DI SEPPIOLINE E CARCIOFI
Warm salad of squid and artichokes

Primi

RAVIOLI ALL'ORTICA IN CREMA
DI GORGONZOLA
Ravioli of nettles with cream of gorgonzola sauce
TORTELLI DI PATATE ALLA MUGELLESE
Tortelli with potato filling

Secondi

FILETTI DI TROTA AFFUMICATA ALLE ERBE
BESCIAMELLA E FORMAGGIO
Smoked Trout fillets with herbs, bechamel and cheese
INSALATA GENOVESE
Salad with walnuts, anchovies and herb pesto
STRUDEL DI VERDURA CON PUREE
DI SCALOGNO
Vegetable strudel with purée of shallots

Dolci

DOLCE AL CIOCCOLATO DI VIRGINIO
Chocolate cake with sesame cream
TORTA DI RICOTTA
Cake of ricotta

OTTORINO

Via delle Oche 12/16
Tel. 215151
Closed: Sun
Credit Cards: All
Reservations: Not necessary
Price: High moderate

COOL AND SPACIOUS

Let's suppose you're near the Duomo and the heat of a sweltering Florentine summer is rapidly sapping your will to go on.

How does this sound: A spacious air-conditioned restaurant with a clean modern wooden interior within the high vaults of an ancient tower, fresh linen and fresh cut flowers on the tables, a battery of waiters on hand, a large interesting menu of first rate Tuscan and Italian dishes, and cold wines with ice buckets to keep them that way. You pay a little more here, but it's worth it, especially if this is the kind of fix your system needs. The tower above Ottorino is one of the city's oldest. Important Florentine families have lived here for over 1000 years.

Thumbs up for the Venetian risotto with black ink squid. The idea of eating white rice blackened by a squid's ink pouch is inherently appealing. Here it's also very tasty, with the right amount of fishiness and a hint of butter.

If you've wanted to try the fried zucchini flowers, this is a good place to order them. Light, fresh and crisp. The macedonia fruit salad comes in a juice of oranges, lemons and white wine. It's the right thing before heading back out to the hot streets. Choice of about 100 wines, the reds mostly from Tuscany, the whites from the Veneto. Good selection of fish, always fresh.

Antipasti

PESCE MISTO
Mixed fish
AVOCADO CON GAMBERETTI
Avocado with shrimp

Primi

RISOTTO NERO CON SEPPIE
Risotto of black ink squid
ZUPPA DI COZZE
Mussel soup
RIGATONI POMODORO E BASILICO
Rigatoni pasta with tomato and basil

Secondi

GIRELLO DI VITELLA AL VINO BIANCO
E FUNGHI
Rump of young beef with white wine and mushrooms
PETTI DI POLLO ALLA PIZZAIOLA E SPINACI
Breast of chicken with tomato, cheese and spinach
TROTA AL BURRO E SALVIA
Trout in butter and sage
MELANZANE ALLA PARMIGIANA
Eggplant baked with cheese and tomato

Dolci

CARRELLO DI DOLCI
Assorted cakes and puddings
MACEDONIA
Fruit salad with white wine

LE MOSSACCE

Via del Proconsolo 55
Tel: 294361
Closed: Sat/Sun
Credit Cards: All
Reservations: No
Price: Inexpensive

"RUDE", CHEAP AND GOOD

Mossacce is a quintessential hole-in-the-wall Florentine trattoria, active for over 100 years yet almost hidden among all the other doors found along Via del Proconsolo. The name means "brusque" or "rude" because of the way the waiters urge you out the door as soon as you are done eating. A restaurant as cheap as this depends on a brisk turnover to make ends meet.

A narrow corridor brings you to a small room that is half kitchen, half dining room. Maneuvering space is limited and at peak hours the heroic waiters become plate-toting contortionists to get everybody served. The tables are laid with butcher paper and there is usually a flask of red wine on the table and ready to pour. You pay only for what you drink. The pastas are substantial. The meat dishes are a good value.

Antipasti

CROSTINI TOSCANI
Tuscan liver paté on bread slices

Primi

CANNELLONI
Tubes of pasta stuffed with meat and cheese
RIGATONI AL RAGU'
Giant macaroni with ragú
RIBOLLITA
Thick vegetable and bread soup

Secondi

INVOLTINI CON CARCIOFI, PROSCIUTTO
E FORMAGGIO
Veal rolled with artichoke, ham, and cheese
TRIPPA ALLA FIORENTINA
Tripe in tomato sauce
SPEZZATINO ALLA FIORENTINA
Beef chunks stewed in tomato sauce

Dolci

MACEDONIA
Fresh fruit salad
CREME CARAMEL
Caramel Custard

Piedra Del Sol
Mexican/Latin
Via de' Ginori 10/r
Tel: 211427
Closed: Wed
Price: Moderate

Here's the Mexican restaurant so many people have been waiting for. This became the *in spot* for the young the first day it opened. A vast hall can accomodate large crowds, nevertheless you had better book ahead to be sure of a table. Tends to get noisy later in the evening. Insist that your food is piping hot, merely tepid Mexican food fails to charm.

Trattoria Za Zà
Piazza del Mercato Centrale
Tel: 215411
Closed: Sun
  Nice, lively market trattoria. Moderate prices.

Gershwin (Persian/Italian)
Via Alfani 26/ red
Tel.:2341606
Closed: Open every day

New restaurant offering both Persian and Italian dishes.

Da Marino all'Ombra del Cupolone
Via Canonica 1/r
Tel: 210285
Closed: Mon

Il Caminetto
Via dello Studio 34
Tel: 296274
Closed: Tues/Wed

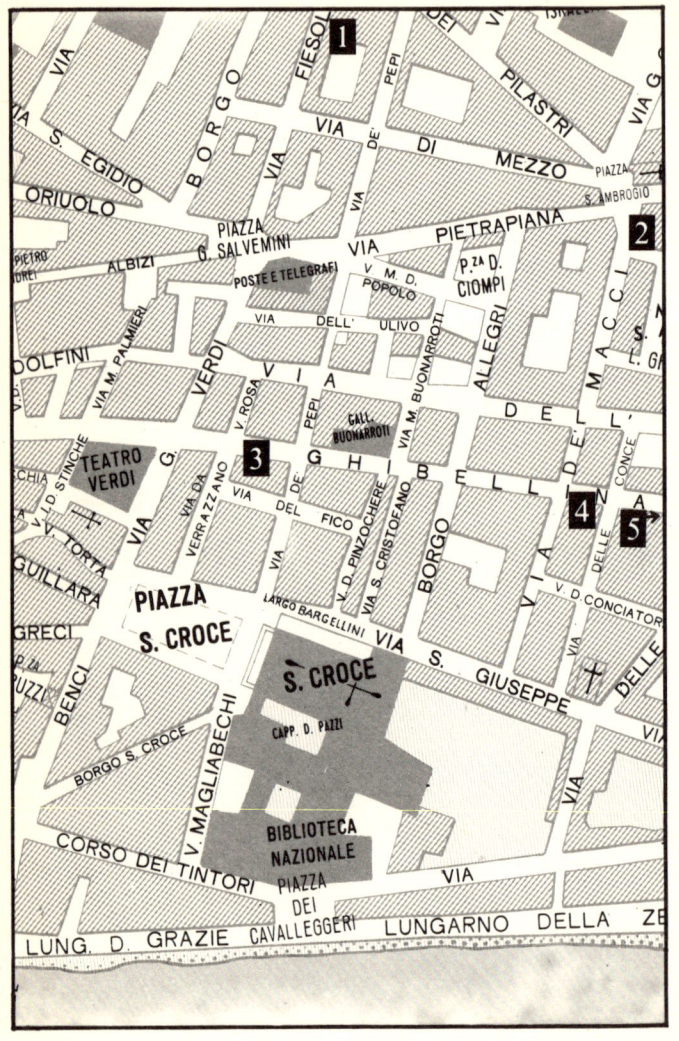

SANTA CROCE

This medieval Franciscan church with frescoes by Giotto contains the tombs of Dante, Michelangelo, Machiavelli, Rossini, Galileo and others.

1. **DA NOI**

2. **CIBREO**

3. **ENOTECA PINCHIORRI**

4. **LA BARAONDA**

5. **DINO**

DA NOI

Via Fiesolana 56 r
Tel: 242917
Closed: Lunch; Sun/Mon; Aug/Xmas
Credit cards: No
Reservations: Necessary
Price: Expensive

LIKE THEIR OWN HOME

Dining for the first time in the intimate space created by Da Noi (which means "at our place") I felt possessed by a kind of restrospective clairvoyance. It was as if I had been present when the husband and wife team of Bruno Tramontana and Sabine Busch first dreamed up this special restaurant. "We'll have just a few tables, in a room of understated charm. It will be like the dining room of our own home". In any case, this describes how their restaurant comes across today. Da Noi is a very personalized establishment without any ostentation. In the kitchen Bruno works with Paulino Casu preparing memorable dishes based on, or inspired by, Tuscan cooking. These dishes, essentially simple in the Tuscan manner, with the ingredients themselves shining out, are often given a creative twist, as a glance at the menu will bear out.

The pastas are homemade, the soups flavorful and often unusual, and the crepes stuffed with good things. The main dishes, which make especially good use of fish and poultry, are cooked with a light hand and often scented with herbs, spices and wines.

Swedish-born Sabine Busch is capable of explaining the menu in a variety of languages and will be glad to help you choose a wine from a superb list. She is acclaimed for her wonderful desserts, one of her secrets being to go light on the sugar.

Reservations must be made well in advance. Da Noi is not open for lunch.

Antipasti

TERRINA DI PESCE CON SALSA ARANCIO
Terrine of fish with orange sauce
PAPPA AL POMODORO
Thick bread and tomato soup

Primi

TAGLIATELLE DI NERO DI SEPPIA
Tagliatelle with black ink of squid
MACCHERONI APERTI DI RADICCHIO ROSSO E PANCETTA
Open macaroni w/ radicchio, smocked bacon, pecorino
SPAGHETTI SALSA DI NASELLONI
Spaghetti with cod sauce

Secondi

SALMONE FARCITO DI PESCE E VERDURE (SALSA DI SPUMANTE)
Salmon stuffed with fish and vegetables (spumante sauce)
GAMBERONI SALSA PEPERONI GIALLI
Shrimp with yellow pepper sauce
CONIGLIO CON CREMA DI BASILICO E MENTA
Rabbit with cream of basil and mint
PICCIONE CON SALSA DI FEGATO DI PICCIONE
Pigeon with sauce of pigeon livers

Dolci

BAVARESE DI RICOTTA
Bavarian pudding of ricotta
GELATO DELLA CASA
Homemade ice-cream

CIBREO

Via dei Macci 18/r
Tel. 2341100
Closed: Sun/Mon; Aug
Credit Cards: All
Reservations: Rest. necessary/Tratt. not necessary
Price: Rest. expensive/Tratt. moderate

RUSTIC DISHES WITH STYLE (NO PASTA)

The wife and husband team of Benedetta and Fabio Picchi have scored a huge success with their restaurant Cibreo, now in its 11th year. What they offer is a refined return to old Tuscan cooking, specializing in traditional dishes which are no longer practical for people to cook at home.

At Cibreo you are greeted with a glass of white wine and a series of interesting appetizers as a welcoming gift. Fabio will then come to your table to dicuss the dishes on offer that day.

A delicious primo, by now a Cibreo standard, is Passato di Peperoni, a purée of yellow peppers, delicate and tasty. Another is the Pappa al Pomodoro, the traditional Florentine dish of bread, tomato, garlic and basil which at Cibreo is such a fragrant concoction that even the real men in your party will relish its baby food texture. The meat and fish dishes are all interesting and beautifully presented.

Cibreo is possibly the only Italian restaurant in the world that doesn't serve pasta. Originally the rationale was that Fabio didn't want to serve anything whose preparation he hadn't personally supervised. Since he also likes to work the floor and kibitz with guests when he's in the mood, pasta dishes became problematical, a non-starter you might say, as they require a good deal of on-the-spot attention if they are going to come out just right. By now Cibreo is so well-known for not serving pasta that Fabio, who definitely has a streak of the mischievous free-spirit in him, is thinking he should cross everyone up and start serving it. (The new Cibreo in Tokyo, which uses 100% Tuscan ingredients flown in daily, does serve pasta. Presumably the Japanese would have considered it a bad joke to be deprived of the quintessential Italian food).

A nice egalitarian touch is the fact that Cibreo is really two eating places separated by a single kitchen. In the main room your meal comes with trimmings and amenities. In a much smaller room called Trattoria Cibreo, which opens onto the Piazza Ambrogio, the fare is much the same as in the 'rich' section, but the service, comforts, portions and prices are all reduced.

The Picchis have recently opened a Cibreo Cafe across the street put together from a variety of unrelated antique parts. The Cafe serves quick, inexpensive lunches and is gaining a reputation as a place to spend lighthearted evening hours, especially if a piano player shows up.

Antipasti

INSALATA DI TRIPPA
Cold tripe salad
POMODORI AL FORNO
Baked tomatoes

Primi

PASSATO DI PEPERONI
Yellow pepper purée
SFORMATO DI SPINACI
Crustless spinach quiche
PAPPA AL POMODORO
Tuscan tomato, garlic and bread soup

Secondi

FILETTO DI SOGLIOLA
Fillet of sole in green onion sauce
COLLO DI POLLO RIPIENO
Chicken neck stuffed with sausage
COSCIO DI AGNELLO DISOSSATO
Leg of lamb de-boned

Dolci

TORTA DI LEMONE
Lemon tart
PERE COTTE AL VINO ROSSO
Pears cooked in red wine
BAVARESE DI VANIGLIA
Vanilla Bavarian cream with Raspberry sauce

ENOTECA PINCHIORRI

Via Ghibellina 87/r
Tel. 242777
Closed: Sun/Mon lunch and August
Credit cards: Amex/Visa
Reservations: Necessary
Price: Expensive

A PEAK OF ITALIAN EXTRAVAGANCE

Signor Pinchiorri expresses concern about the amount of misinformation loose on the subject of eating out. So let us be perfectly clear. The Enoteca Pinchiorri is not just another luxury restaurant; rather, it is meant to provide a gastronomic happening of extravagant proportions.

First, there's the setting. In a 15th century Florentine palazzo we are surrounded by Ginori china, Riedel crystal, a variety of silver accessories, damask tablecloths, antique furniture, fine paintings and expensive bouquets of flowers. In other words, nothing but the best. The waiters are attired in tuxedoes, even at lunchtime, and they perform with panache. Summertime dining is shifted to an open-air courtyard bursting with greenery and cut flowers.

It is all primarily a showcase for one of the finest collections anywhere of French, Italian, and Californian wines. Signor Pinchiorri developed a passion for fine wines when still a youngster. Today his 'winelist' runs to three volumes. A tour of the riches in the Pinchiorri wine cellar is said to reduce wine connoisseurs to utter submission. While the prices may seem astronomical to novices, old hands agree that the Pinchiorri wines are very fairly priced, with a minimum of mark-up.

All of this puts terrific pressure on Annie Feolde in the kitchen. A Frenchwoman who came to Florence 21 years ago to study Italian, she is faced with the daunting task of providing dishes that can hold their own with the battery of superlatives the Enoteca throws at you. (Not that she came totally unprepared for such a mission: her cousins are the Haeberlins, owner-chefs of l'Auberge de l'Ill in Alsace). Ms. Feolde has accepted the challenge with humility, pluck, and hard work. Over the years she has become a brilliant chef.

Annie Feolde offers three complete menus which change with the seasons. One is a meal entirely of fish. Another is called Tuscany Rediscovered and consists of dishes from old Tuscan recipes which Annie has meticulously researched. The third menu is called Creative Cuisine and offers a series of Annie's own culinary inventions. All three menus are designed to harmonize with a series of superb wines sampled during the course of the meal.

Regarding the authenticity of her cuisine Ms. Feolde has this to say. "People know I'm French and assume that I put a French accent on all the dishes. It's not true. Nobody tries to be more Tuscan than I do. The recipes* for Skewered Shrimps and Red Mullet with Porcini Mushrooms are purely Tuscan and I have left them exactly as I found them, except for some refinements of technique. See if you can find these dishes anywhere else in Tuscany today".

The complete meals run around $100 each and, all things considered, offer good value. There is also an à la carte menu. The wines start at about $45, and go up to the $200 range, unless you want something really special.

* *See recipes*

Antipasti

RAGU' DI FASOLARI AL BASILICO CON VELLUTATA DI PEPERONE
Smooth Venus clams and basil in a red pepper sauce
SPIEDINO DI CODA DI ROSPO CON POMODORO, PANCETTA E CIPOLLE CROCCANTI
Roasted Angler fish with tomato, bacon and crispy onions
SOFFIATO DI GAMBERI IN SALSA CROSTACEI E JULIENNE DI TARTUFO
Shrimp soufflet with shellfish sauce and chopped truffles
BACCALA CON I CECI
Salt cod with chick peas

Primi

RAVIOLI DI BRANZINO ARROSTO CON FINOCCHIO, SALSA PICCANTE DI TRIGLIE
Ravioli filled with roast sea bass and fennel red-mullet sauce
CANNELLONI AL GORGONZOLA E NOCI TRITATE
Gorgonzola and chopped walnuts cannelloni
ACQUACOTTA
Mushrooms and egg in vegetable broth

Secondi

PETTO DI PICCIONE AL VINO ROSSO E PEPERONCINO CON VENTAGLIO DI PERA
Pigeon breast in red wine and hot pepper sauce (served with cooked pear)
FILETTO DI AGNELLO IMPANATO AI FUNGHI PORCINI CON PATATE FRITTE
Breaded lamb chops with porcini mushrooms and potatoes fried in truffle-flavored olive oil
CIBREO CON FEGATINI, ROGNONI E CRESTE DI GALLO
Old Tuscan dish of cock's liver and comb in a slightly hot sauce

Dolci
CREMA DI PROCOPIO NEL CONO
Procope's coffee ice cream in a special cone.

La Baraonda

Via Ghibellina 67/r
Tel. 2341171
Closed: Sun/Holidays/Aug
Credit cards: Amex, Diners
Reservations: Advisable
Price: High moderate

A PASSION FOR AUTHENTICITY

To the owners of the Baraonda the most welcome compliment of all is the nostalgic crooning of middle-aged Florentines. "We haven't tasted these dishes since our grandmothers cooked for us years ago". The Baraonda was born with one aim in mind: to re-create the dishes of genuine Tuscan home cooking of a bygone age.

Duccio and Elena Magni are relatively new to the restaurant business having opened the Baraonda just 4 years ago.

The Magnis are quick to direct the interested visitor to their culinary Bible, *The Art of the Kitchen*, by Artusi, first printed in 1860. Artusi's book is an ardent, even mystical, discourse on Tuscan cooking methods, some of which were in use before the Renaissance. One point clearly asserts itself: the essence of authentic Tuscan cooking is long and loving preparation in the style of Tuscan grandmothers. "To appreciate us", says Duccio, "one should understand what we offer, and what we don't offer. As good as they are, grilled meats, including the Florentine beefsteak, are not in our repertoire, nor is anything related to nouvelle cuisine or inventive cooking, nor a single dish not historically Tuscan".

Fish only on Fridays, and then only the freshwater baccalà (cod) since in the old days fresh fish from the sea was naturally never to be found in Florence. The only cheese offered is a Tuscan pecorino. Virtually everything served at the Baraonda is prepared on the premises, from the home-made pastas to the desserts and liqueurs. The wine list is exclusively Tuscan and features the new super vini da tavola (see chapter on Tuscan wines). Duccio is presently finishing the third year of a rigorous three year course which will qualify him as an expert in Italian wines.

Antipasti

SALSA DI OLIVE NERE CON SCHIACCIATINE
Black olive paste with flat bread

Primi

RISOLATA
Rice cooked with romaine lettuce
TAGLIATELLE AL RAGU ALLA FIORENTINA
Pasta with ragù of beef and mushrooms
FARINATA DI CAVOLO NERO
Thick soup of black cabbage and corn meal

Secondi

POLPETTONE IN UMIDO
Meatloaf cooked in seasoned tomato sauce
FRANCESINA
Pieces of beef cooked with onions and white wine
SFORMATO DI CARCIOFI CON SALSA DI FUNGHI
PORCINI E FEGATINI DI POLLO
Artichoke soufflè with sauce of porcini mushrooms
and chicken liver
ROGNONCINI DI VITELLA AL VINO BIANCO
Veal kidney cooked in flour, parsley and white wine

Dolci

TORTA DI MELE ALLA BARAONDA
Carmeled cross between apple cake and apple pie
SPUMONE AL CIOCCOLATO
Chocolate mousse
SORBETTO ALLA FRUTTA
Fruit sorbet

DINO

Via Ghibellina 51
Tel. 241452
Closed: Sun eve/Mon and August
Credit Cards: Amex, Diners, Visa, Eurocard
Reservations: Advisable
Price: High moderate

RECIPES FROM THE MEDICI PRINCES

Dino Casini is a Florentine whose love of Tuscan food and lively interest in Renaissance history has produced a restaurant of special interest located on the edge of the Santa Croce district in a 14th century palazzo.

The specialities of the house are based on recipes the Medici used for their banquets. A page of Dino's menu - in Italian - is dedicated to a discussion of the origins and ingredients of these dishes. Here are some samples.

Stracotto del Granduca
"From our research conducted in the Mugello valley, we've discovered that during the Medicean feasts the custom was to choose the best piece of beef and flavor it with garlic, rosemary, almonds, pine nuts, mint and cinnamon... and to finish cooking the dish with the best Chianti available. This is how we prepare our long-cooked beef which we've dedicated to the Grand Duke".

Filetto di Maiale al Cartoccio
"Modern method for cooking a pork fillet flavored with traditional spices and wrapped in an envelope of aluminum foil."

Coscio di Vitella al Mirto
"The best piece of lean veal that we can find. Cooked in a traditional oven and flavoured with the addition of myrtle".

Dino's is strictly family. Signora Casini runs the kitchen while son Massimo and daughter Sonia work the floor. The wine list is ample and reasonably priced.

Antipasti

INSALATINA DELLA CORTE DEI MEDICI
Salad from the Medici court
FILETTO DI VITELLA AFFUMICATO
Smoked veal fillet

Primi

RISOTTO DELLA RENZA
Risotto with herbs
SPAGHETTI ALLA DINO
Spaghetti in vegetable sauce
ZUPPA DI CIPOLLE
Tuscan onion soup

Secondi

GARRETTO GHIBELLINO
Pig shin cooked with celery, sage and other vegetables
COSCIO DI VITELLA AL MIRTO
Lean veal slice, oven baked with myrtle
FILETTO DI MAIALE AL CARTOCCIO
Spiced pork baked in foil paper

Dolci

MACEDONIA DI FRUTTA ESOTICA
Exotic fruit salad
PRUGNE COTTE NEL VINO CHIANTI
Prunes cooked in Chianti wine

ALESSI
Via di Mezzo 26 red
Tel. 41821
Price: Inexpensive

To accomodate the office workers in the neighborhood who are restricted to short lunch breaks, Signor Alessi, a food historian, serves up his special authentic Tuscan dishes in record time and for prices one can make a habit of. Plan to adapt to the faster pace.

DANNY ROCK
Via Pandolfini 13/r
Tel: 2340307
Closed: Mon

Danny Rock is a new, New York City-style restaurant which aimed at the younger crowd and scored a direct hit. The Danny Rock hamburger is presented a' l'Americana and is excellent by anybody's standards. It's served with french fries.

The Crepes, on the other hand, are usually made by a Frenchman named Laurent. They come either savoury or sweet. Substantial salads are also on offer. Videos overhead play classic cartoons, or skiing segments. The downstairs room is to be avoided when full as it gets unbearably noisy.

QUINTO
Piazza dei Peruzzi 5
Tel. 213323
Closed: Mon

The only restaurant we know of in Florence where you can hear Neapolitan songs and Italian arias live, sometimes sung by Quinto himself.

Cuscussu
Via L. C. Farina, 2/r
Tel. 241890
Closed: Sat/Sun eve
Kosher Specialties
Price: Moderate

On Tuesday evenings you'll find a long table replete with some 20 platters of Jewish and Asian dishes. Thursday evenings are given over to international Jewish dishes.

Mr. Hang (Chinese)
Via Ghibellina 134
Tel: 2344810
Closed: Monday

I can report that in making the rounds I encountered many Florentine restaurant owners enthusiastic about Mr. Hang. Overworked as most of them are, they've even discovered the joys of Chinese take out. There are now something like 20 Chinese restaurants in Florence. Mr. Hang is generally considered the best of the bunch.

La Maremma
Via G. Verdi 16
Tel. 244615
Closed: Wed/Thu

Nice family run place. Menu rather too large.

La Maremmana
Via dei Macci 77/r
Tel. 241226
Closed: Sun

Known for very good value. "Si mangia bene, e si spende poco". (You eat well, and you spend little). Usually offers very fairly priced tourist meal.

ALLE MURATE
Via Ghibellina 52/r
Tel. 240618
Closed: Mon

This restaurant, which has a sister establishment in New York City, is known for creative cooking.

I' FRANCESCANO
Via S. Giuseppe 26
Tel. 241605
Closed: Wed (Open only evenings)

Amazing following of young people who flood in around 9:30 in the evening or later. If you come early, or at lunchtime, you can have the place to yourself and eat very well.

NATALINO
Borgo degli Albizi 17/r
Tel: 253404
Closed: Sun

Includes a beautiful room with fresco by the young Romano Stefanelli, the artist featured on our cover.

OSTERIA BARCACCIA
Via de' Lavatoi 3
Tel: 283958
Closed: Mon/Tue

TRATTORIA PALLOTTINO
Via Isola delle Stinche 1/red
Tel. 289573
Closed: Monday and Tuesday lunch

LA VIE EN ROSE
Borgo Allegri 68r
Tel: 245860
Closed: Tue
Fine creative dishes, both Tuscan and French.
High moderate.

TIRABUSCIO
Via dei Benci 34
Tel. 2476225
Closed: Monday

DEL FAGIOLI
Corso dei Tintori 47
Tel. 244285
Closed: Sat/Sun

I GOLOSI
Via Pandolfini 13
Closed: Mon

PIAZZA DELLA SIGNORIA

Superb piazza at the Palazzo Vecchio, Florence's city hall. This is where the citizens of the first modern democracy came to vote with their voices.

1. **P**ENNELLO

2. **O**STERIA **G**ANINO

3. **A**CQUA **A**L **D**UE

4. **I'**CHE C'È C'È

5. **M**ONKEY **B**USINESS

PENNELLO (CASA DI DANTE)

Via Dante Alighieri 4
Tel: 294848
Closed: Sun eve/Mon and August
Credit cards: No
Reservations: Advisable
Price: Moderate

LAST OF A BREED

This is a surviving old-style Florentine trattoria next door to Dante's house that dates back to 1500 when painter/artist Mariotto Albertinelli opened Pennello (which means paintbrush) to share wine and good times with Michelangelo, Benvenuto Cellini and other members of the artistic crowd. The fare is still geared to Everyman's pocketbook, a pleasant find in the center of historic Florence. The surroundings are simple and deeply Tuscan, with a mixed-bag of paintings on the walls, and no dearth of wise-cracking waiters.

The most visible feature of Pennello is the vast assortment of antipasti on a central table including every sort of marinated fish, shellfish, vegetable, and salad.
That light, but interesting lunch so many over-fed travelers are looking for can be easily assembled from the vast offerings found on the antipasti table. Just add some bread and a glass of wine, and you are all set until evening.

The rest of the menu is strictly Tuscan. On Fridays the traditional baccalà - salt cod cooked with tomatoes and garlic.

Antipasti

A large selection of fish and vegetable antipasti, with an equal number of sauces.

Primi

SPAGHETTI ALLA CARRETTIERA
Spaghetti in a spicy tomato sauce
TORTELLONI ALLA PANNA
Tortellini with cream
RISOTTO ORTOLANA
Vegetable risotto

Secondi

BISTECCA ALLA FIORENTINA
Grilled Florentine beefsteak
AGNELLO AL FORNO
Roasted lamb

SCAMPI E DENTICI
Shrimp and dentex (a Mediterranean fish)

Dolci

MERINGA
Meringue cake
MACEDONIA
Fruit salad

OSTERIA GANINO

Piazza dei Cimatori 4
Tel: 214125
Closed: Sun
Credit cards: Yes
Reservations: Advisable
Price: High Moderate

GREAT FRIED FOOD IN THE PIAZZETTA

This small, first-rate trattoria is one of the most popular spots in town, especially among the young hip set. The Florentine soccer team frequents Ganino, as well as artists, journalists and the like.

Ganino's specialty is fried foods. The full plate is a succulent mix of fried rabbit, chicken, brain, vegetables and apple. All kinds of seasonal vegetables are likely to come fried as well, including zucchini flowers and tomatoes.

The pastas are strictly fresh and lean heavily on sauces of porcini mushrooms and truffles. These sauces are of a rich consistency that will have you insisting that the dish contains cream. In fact, no cream is used. For a second course not-of-meat try grilled porcini mushrooms with the fragrant Tuscan herb *nipitella*.

Ganino's outdoor seating in the small piazzetta in front of the restaurant is blissfully protected from motor traffic. A table here, with a pitcher of sparkling house rosé, is gold on a steamy summer evening.

Antipasti

CROSTINI
Tuscan pate' on toast

Primi

STROZZAPRETI STRASCICATI
Fresh eggless pasta fusilli with ragu
TAGLIATELLE PORCINI O TARTUFI
Tagliatelle with porcini mushrooms or truffles

Secondi

FRITTO MISTO - CONIGLIO, POLLI, CERVELLO E VERDURE
Mixed fried foods: rabbit, chicken, brain and seasonal vegetables
PORCINI ALLA GRIGLIA CON NIPITELLA
Grilled porcini mushrooms with wild herb
BISTECCA ALLA FIORENTINA
Grilled Florentine beefsteak

Dolci

TIRAMISU'
Cake and cream cheese pudding

ACQUA AL DUE

Via della Vigna Vecchia 40/r
Tel: 284170
Closed: Mon
Credit cards: No
Reservations: Necessary
Price: Moderate

CAN'T DECIDE ? TASTE THEM ALL

If you arrive at the usual dining hours you may find the doorway blocked by people waiting to be seated. Acqua al Due is especially popular for its *assaggi,* or tastes. These are a series of small portions to taste, available for the antipasti, first dishes and dolci. A wide selection of appetizing salads may be hard to pass up.

The selection of *assaggi* is a good way to deal with a craving for pasta, especially if you're indecisive about which sauce to choose. Standard sauces include mushroom, spinach and cream, and four cheeses.

You can follow the same procedure with the sweets which are excellent. This double series of tasting portions is a starchy way to go, but presumably you'll walk it off finding your way around Florence. The meat dishes are good, too. Breast of chicken is perhaps the first choice.

Antipasti

INSALATE VARIE
Various salads

Primi

RISOTTO DI SPINACI
Spinach risotto
TAGLIATELLE AI FUNGHI PORCINI
Tagliatelle with porcini mushrooms
TOPINI AL GORGONZOLA
Gnocchi with gorgonzola cheese
FARFALLINE AL SALMONE
Butterfly pasta with salmon

Secondi

PETTI DI POLLO
Chicken breast
COUS-COUS D'AGNELLO
Lamb cous-cous
LOMBATINA AL PEPE VERDE
Veal steak with hot green peppers

Dolci

SELEZIONI DI TORTE
Varied cakes and puddings

I CHE C'È C'È

Via Magalotti 11/red
Tel: 216589
Closed: Mon
Credit cards: No
Reservations: Not necessary
Price: Moderate

WHAT THERE IS, THERE IS.

"What there is, there is" is an approximation of the Florentine expression *i che c'è c'è*. Be advised that there is always something cooking here off the menu. Ask your waiter what the cook has special in the kitchen. It may just be something like ravioli in white truffle sauce.

Chef Gino Noci is a Florentine with a long and varied career in the restaurant business, including a stint in a French restaurant in London. His pleasant restaurant tucked in among the narrow streets between Piazza Signoria and Santa Croce caters to lawyers from the nearby courthouse, artists, assorted locals and of course the tourists who find their way here. Signor Noci emphasizes that his establishment is a place for friends to meet and pass the time, a restaurant as public house.

But don't think there's anything common about the food here. Gino's a pro who serves only top quality dishes. You will be well looked after by two young waiters, Riccardo and Jacopo, anxious to use their English.

Antipasti

CROSTINI ALLA GINO (DI CARCIOFI, FUNGHI, FEGATO)
Crostini of artichokes, mushrooms, liver paté
BUFFET: SALAMI, VASSOI CON INSALATE DI MARE
Buffet: cured meats, seafood salads

Primi

RIBOLLITA
Tuscan bread, bean and cabbage soup
ZUPPA DI FARRO
Grain (emmer) soup
PENNE STRASCICATE ALLA FIORENTINA
Penne (macaroni) in meat sauce
TAGLIATELLE CON FUNGHI
Tagliatelle with mushroom sauce

Secondi

SALSICCE E FAGIOLI
Sausage and beans
STRACOTTO ALLA FIORENTINA
Pot roast in a tomato sauce
CONIGLIO RIPIENO
Egg and spinach wrapped in rabbit meat
LOMBATA DI MANZO ALLA BRACE
Grilled beefsteak

Dolci

TIRAMISU'
Mascarpone cheese sweetened with sugar and liquor
PANNA COTTA
Florentine cooked cream

MONKEY BUSINESS

Chiasso dei Baroncelli
Piazza della Signoria
Tel: 288219
Closed: Tues
Credit cards: Visa, MC, Amex, Diners
Reservation: Advisable
Price: Expensive

CHIC JUNGLE SETTING

A few steps from the Ponte Vecchio, but hidden in a back alley, is a new and improbable restaurant on the Florentine scene. Luciano Ioppoli, a professional restaurateur, is banking on his exotic theme restaurant wherein a life-sized paper mache' elephant stands amid potted palms and walls frescoed with jungle scenes. An American-style bar and a separate piano bar adjoin two dining rooms in a spacious Florentine palazzo complete with vaulted ceilings and Grecian columns.

By Florentine standards the menu is as exotic as the decor. Traditional dishes are flavored with oriental spices such as ginger and soya. A thoroughly satisfying example of the way Monkey Business handles cross-cultural culinary matings is the appetizer of Tuscan white beans, cuttlefish and zucchini with a pinch of hot chili pepper. The giant prawns with ginger, soya and pistacchio sauce are excellent; the strong flavors of the sauce are muted and do not overwhelm the shrimp.

The menu also includes traditional Italian dishes to accomodate cautious native palates and travelers who, when in Italy, would prefer an interesting ravioli. Signor Ioppoli is building an impressive wine list. He is also riding the vanguard of the movement which provides smokeless dining rooms, still a radically new concept in Italy.

Antipasti

SOFFIATO DI PARMIGIANO IN SALSA FONDUTA
Pastry with melted parmesan
BRESAOLA CON PUREE TIEPIDO AL ROSMARINO
Seasoned beef with puree' of rosemary

Primi

RISOTTO ALLA BRUNELLESCHI
(con funghi prosciutto cotto in salsa di asparagi)
Mushroom risotto with ham and asparagus sauce
RAVIOLI IN SALSA DI NOCI
Ravioli of spinach and ricotta in walnut sauce

Secondi

FILETTO DEL FIACCHERAIO
Beef fillet with red wine and pepper
CODE DI SCAMPI
Jumbo prawns with ginger and pistacchio sauce
VITELLA CON RUCOLA E CARCIOFI IN FORMA
Veal with rucola and artichokes

Dolci

BAVARESE CON FRUTTA DELLA STAGIONE
Bavarian pudding with fruit
TORTA DI CIOCCOLATA
Chocolate cake

TRATTORIA ANITA
Via Parlascio 2/r
Tel: 218698
Closed: Sun/Wed lunch

Anita's prices are the lowest we know of. The fixed price for a first, second and dessert is around 10,000 lire.

Let's not have illusions about this; there's a limit to what a restaurant can offer for that kind of money. But it can be said that Anita's has always offered good honest fare. (Under new ownership since 1.4.90)

EITO (JAPANESE)
Via dei Neri 72
Tel: 210940
Closed: Mon

When your constitution cries out for a respite from pasta, nothing breaks the pattern quite so refreshingly as a good Japanese meal.

Most of your favorites will be here: sashimi, tempura, baked-eggplant, stewed and marinated beef, cooked salmon. Like Japanese restaurants everywhere, Eito is expensive. The freshness of the fish is everything and that freshness costs.

TRATTORIA ALFREDO
Via dei Leoni 14
Tel: 224912
Closed: Thu

BARGELLO
Piazza della Signoria 4/r
Tel; 214071
Closed: Mon

BUCA POLDI
Chiasso degli Armagnati 2/r
Tel: 296578
Closed: Thu

BUCA SAN FIRENZE
Via Condotta 9/r
Tel: 296804
Closed: Wed

BUZZINO
Via dei Leoni 8/r
Tel: 298013
Closed: Mon

CAVALLINO
Piazza della Signoria 28
Tel: 215818
Closed: Tue

CINQUE AMICI
Via dei Cimatori 30
Tel: 296672
Closed: Sun/Mon

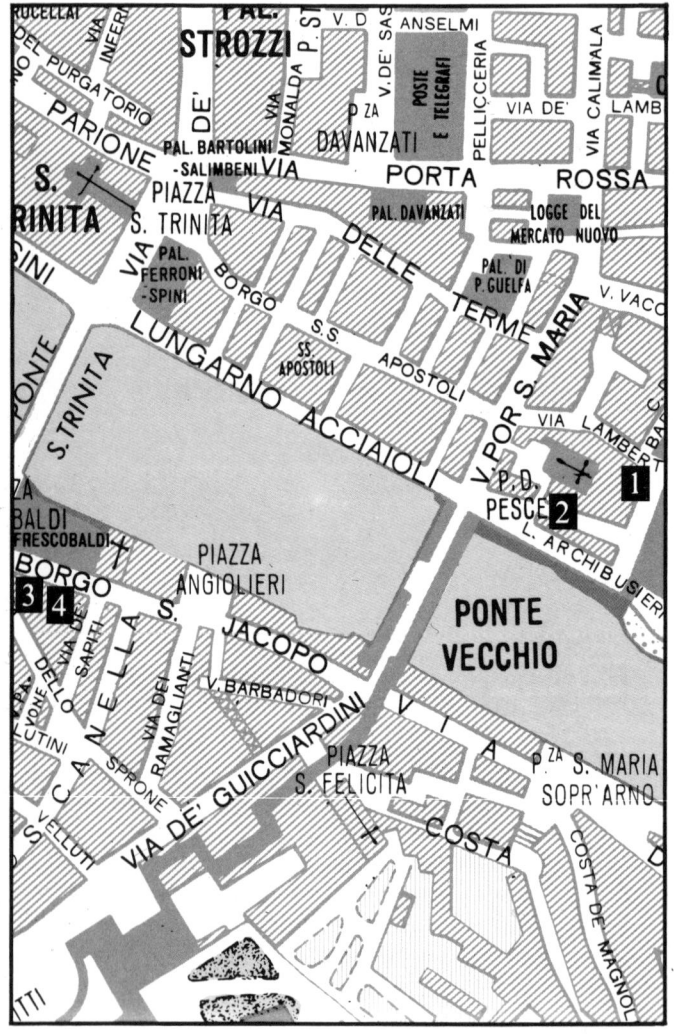

PONTE VECCHIO

The old bridge, piled high with jewelry shops and supporting a stretch of Vasari's Corridor, has survived countless floods and the bombardments of WW 2 since it's construction in 1345.

1. ANTICO FATTORE

2. BUCA DELL'ORAFO

3. CAMMILLO

4. CINGHIALE BIANCO

ANTICO FATTORE

Via Lambertesca 1/red
Tel: 261215 (will become 2381215)
Closed: Sun/Mon: Aug
Credit card: Amex, Visa
Reservations: Not necessary
Price: Moderate

FOOD, TALK, AND LITERARY PRIZES

Chianti Ruffino, one of the largest producers, bottlers and exporters of wine in Italy, offers its own literary awards each year. The winners are invited to receive their prizes over dinner at the Antico Fattore. Most recently the American Pulitzer Prize winner, Peter Taylor, took first prize edging out novelists from Morocco and Spain.

The idea behind associating the awards with a restaurant is to acknowledge the close relationship which exists in Italy between literary production and good eating. Of course, it would be hard to name anything in Italy that doesn't have a close relationship with good eating.

While having a quick lunch here the other day I realized that literature - at least the oral variety - and this trattoria were made for each other. What a lot of talk there is in this place! And how the waiters play to the crowd, tossing off quips and provocations while sauntering across the stage of the central room with bowls of pasta held high. It brings to mind that for a great many Italians mealtime is as much devoted to talk as to food. The Antico Fattore is known for good food, by the way, and we can only hope that its role as bestower of awards for excellence will keep complacency far from the door. The ambience is that of a country trattoria.

Antipasti

MISTO TOSCANO
Crostini, prosciutto and salami

Primi

RIBOLLITA
Vegetable and bread soup
PAPPA AL POMODORO
Thick bread soup of tomato and basil
RIGATONI STRASCICATI
Large macaroni with ragu

Secondi

TRIPPA ALLA FIORENTINA
Tripe with tomato
STRACOTTO
Long-cooked beef with tomato
AGNELLO AL FORNO
Roast lamb

Dolci

MELE E PERE COTTE
Cooked apples and pears
TORTA DELLA NONNA
Cream pie

Buca Dell'Orafo

Volta dei Girolami 28/r
Tel: 213619
Closed: Sun lunch
Credit cards: No
Reservations: Advisable
Price: High moderate

FINE FOOD IN A SMALL CELLAR

This restaurant is half-hidden under an arch just on the Duomo-side of the Ponte Vecchio. *Buca* means hole, and indeed this is a tiny underground place that used to be a goldsmiths workshop. It seats only 35 people at a time.

However, there is nothing dark and dismal about Buca dell'Orafo. It is a cheery place, thanks to the interesting paintings, the spirited banter the waiters lavish on guests, and most of all to the fine food. The pastas are homemade and come with top quality sauces, especially those made from fresh vegetables.

This is another restaurant known for its Florentine beefsteaks. Come to think of it, when a Florentine restaurant is in a cellar and begins with the word Buca, you can bet that it does a good and proper *bistecca*. Most of the paintings are by the eccentric Florentine artist Fosco Pavi who works exclusively in, or very near, Florence to support a stable of some 40 dogs.

Antipasti

FINOCCHIONA
Salami with fennel

Primi

TAGLIATELLE CON FUNGHI
Tagliatelle pasta with mushrooms
TAGLIERINI CON ASPARAGINA
Taglierini pasta with asparagus

Secondi

BOCCONCINI CON CARCIOFI
Meat bits with artichokes
STACOTTO E FAGIOLI
Pot roast with white beans
FRITTO DI SCAMPI
Fried shrimp
MAZZANCOLLE ALLA LIVORNESE
Fish stew Livorno style

Dolci

CASSATA STRACIATELLE
Ice cream cake
FRAGOLINE DI BOSCO
Forest strawberries

CAMMILLO

Borgo San Jacopo 57/r
Tel: 212427
Closed: Wed/Thu
Credit cards: All
Reservations: Advisable
Price: High moderate

THREE GENERATIONS OF HIGH STANDARDS

Cammillo has been a top Florentine trattoria for over three generations. The original owner, Cammillo Masiero, passed the trattoria on to his son Bruno who in turn gave over the reins six years ago to his son, Francesco.

At Cammillo the tone is set by the pleasant commotion of waiters, in white shirts and black bow-ties, getting the job done. Francesco explains that most Italians don't like to wait between courses. Leave the interminable evenings at the table to the French.   Pazienza in all things, except in getting fed. In order to keep everyone's meal moving along at a good clip, a large staff of help is required. Not to worry, at Cammillo you will be well looked after, but never smothered or rushed.

Cammillo offers a mix of Tuscan and classic Italian cuisine with a menu constantly changing to take advantage of the vegetables and meats of the season. Francesco is not shy about trying out something of his own invention. A recent new dish of his is chicken livers with Tuscan white beans: not exactly a glamorous pairing, as he would be the first to admit. Yet nothing is more solidly Tuscan than white beans, and matching them with tender morsels of liver puts them in yet another favorable light.

Cammillo also takes utmost advantage of each season's new vegetables, the *primizie*, getting them on the tables as soon as possible, often in sauces over homemade pasta. The taglierini with fresh early peas and butter is delicious.

Cammillo's prices are a touch high but in explanation Francesco asks you to look around, as much to ask "How can I run the place as I do without charging for it"? The three house wines and the olive oil are produced on the family's farm some 25 kilometres south of Florence. These products are on sale directly to the public.

Antipasti

INSALATA DI PINOLI, RUCOLA E PARMIGIANO
Salad with rucola, pine nuts and parmesan cheese
CARPACCIO TIEPIDO DI SALMONE ALL'ERBA CIPOLLINA
Raw salmon (warmed) with chives

Primi

TAGLIERINI CON PISELLI FRESCHI
Taglierini pasta with fresh peas and butter
MINESTRONE DI VERDURA E DI RISO
Hearty soup with vegetables and rice
TAGLIERINI CON TARTUFO BIANCO
Taglierini pasta with white truffles (Sept - Jan only)

Secondi

AGNELLO CON PISELLI FRESCHI
Lamb with fresh peas
SCAMPI AL CURRY CON RISO
Curried shrimp with rice
SCAMPI ALL'UCCELLETTO
Shrimp with beans in garlic, sage and tomato sauce

Dolci

FRUTTI DI BOSCO CON CREMA
Berries with cream
MERINGA CON CIOCCOLATO
Meringue cake with chocolate

Osteria Del Cinghiale Bianco

Borgo San Jacopo 43/red
Tel: 215706
Closed: Tue/Wed
Credit cards: no
Reservations: Necessary
Price: Moderate

A MEDIEVAL INN *THE WHITE BOAR*

In the 1970's an Englishman named Stephen Tobin opened this charming restaurant taking great pains to retain as much of the medieval architecture as possible. He also added a great many touches of his own to recreate the feel of a medieval inn.

Seven years ago Massimo Masselli bought the restaurant and decided to leave it exactly as it was. Signor Masselli's philosophy is straightforward enough: keep the running of the place in the family to minimize complications, and provide good food at reasonable prices so that the customers keep coming back for more.

The Carabaccia onion soup is made according to the medieval recipe using white wine and cinnamon. It is a thick soup with a strong flavor. Cinghiale means wild boar and if it's boar meat you're looking for, you won't be disappointed. It appears as an appetizer in thin slices of seasoned meat, and in a boar stew served with polenta (corn meal porridge) and black olives. There's good value here, and people do come back for more.

Antipasti

ANTIPASTI DI CINGHIALE
Cold cuts of wild boar
FETTUNTA
Garlic bread with fresh olive oil

Primi

CARABACCIA
Thick onion soup cooked in cinnamon and white wine
STROZZAPRETI AL BURRO
Spinach and ricotta dumplings with butter
MACCHERONCETTI DI PRIMAVERA
Macaroni with fresh spring vegetables

Secondi

CINGHIALE CON POLENTA
Wild boar meat with polenta (corn porridge)
SCALOPPINE CON FUNGHI
Veal scaloppini with mushrooms
BRACIOLINE ALLA PIZZAIOLA
Beef cutlets with tomato and cheese sauce

Dolci

MACEDONIA
Fresh fruit salad
CREM CARAMEL
Caramel custard
CANTUCCINI CON VIN SANTO
Hard almond cookies with sweet wine

MAMA GINA
Borgo S. Jacopo 37/r
Tel: 296O09
(will become 2396009)
Closed: Sun

A fine typical Tuscan trattoria.

AL LUME DI CANDELA
Via Terme 23/r
Tel: 294566
Closed: Sun

By candlelight is the name of this intimate, expensive restaurant.

LA SAGRESTIA
Via Giucciardini 27/r
Tel: 210003
Closed: Mon

Relatively new restaurant. Wide selection of dishes, both Italian and International. The wine list is as wide as the menu.

SANTA TRINITA (Via Tornabuoni)

The beautiful bridge of Santa Trinita (where legend says Dante and Beatrice met for the first time) leads to the piazza and church of Santa Trinita and to the shoppers row of Via Tornabuoni.

1. BUCA LAPI

2. CANTINETTA ANTINORI

3. BELLE DONNE

4. COCO LEZZONE

5. DONEY

6. TOULA

BUCA LAPI

Via del Trebbio 1/r
Tel: 213768
Closed: Tue
Credit cards: All
Reservations: Advisable
Price: High moderate

BISTECCA IN THE WINE CELLAR

Buca Lapi occupies the cellars of the Palazzo Antinori where wine from the Antinori farms was stored and sold to the Florentine public as long ago as the early 1500's. In 1880, the cellars became a restaurant taking the name of the cellarkeeper, Signor Lapi.

Buca Lapi is a serious establishment proud of being one of the oldest Florentine restaurants still in operation. Appropriately enough, the specialty here is the traditional Florentine beefsteak grilled quickly over searing coals in the prescribed manner. All the Antinori wines are on hand - a Chianti Riserva is the usual recommendation to accompany the bistecca - as well as a selection of Italy's best. The waiters are numerous and smartly attired in bow ties and vests. They prepare a salad dressing at your table with a dexterity rarely seen these days. The trolley of antipasti is artfully arranged. There is a sweet trolley as well.

For some reason the entire restaurant, ceilings included, is papered with old travel posters. I suppose there's always the chance that a brilliant travel idea will present itself between courses.

Antipasti

PROSCIUTTO E MELONE
Prosciutto and cantaloupe
CROSTINI TOSCANI
Mixed crostini

Primi

CANNELLONI
Canelloni
RAVIOLI AL RAGU'
Fresh ravioli with ragú
PENNETTE AL SALMONE
Penne with salmon, tomato and cream

Secondi

BISTECCA ALLA FIORENTINA
Florentine steak charcoal grilled
LOMBATINA ALLA LAPI
Veal steak
COSCIOTTO DI AGNELLO
Leg of lamb

Dolci

ZUCCOTTO
Ice cream cake
ZUPPA ALLE MANDORLE
Almond cream cake

CANTINETTA ANTINORI

Piazza Antinori 3
Tel: 292234
Closed: Sat/Sun/holidays; August
Credit cards: Amex
Reservations: Advisable
Price: Expensive

THE ANTINORI WINE BAR-RESTAURANT

Located in the beautiful Palazzo Antinori (in Piazza Antinori) this wine-bar restaurant serves as a showcase for the full array of Antinori wines. The Antinori family has been making wines for over 600 years and is today about the most respected name in the business, thanks largely to the magic touch of Giacomo Tachis who directs the wine-making operations in nearby San Casciano.

At the Cantinetta you can order by the glass most of the vaunted Antinori wines, such as the Chianti Riserva, Tignanello and Solaia. Descriptions are provided to give you a feel for what the wines are all about.

The food is based on Tuscan cuisine and includes excellent cheeses produced on the Antinori farms. The accent is on light dishes. The wine bar provides an opportunity to do some serious wine tasting or to have a glass of fine wine as an apperitivo before going on to dinner.

Antipasti

FETTUNTA CON CAVOLO NERO
Toasted country bread with black cabbage
CROSTONE AL FORMAGGIO
Toast with cheese

Primi

RISOTTO AGLI SCAMPI
Prawn risotto
FETTUCCINE ALLE OLIVE
Fettuccine in black olive sauce

Secondi

INSALATA DI PESCE FRESCO E FAGIOLI
Fresh seafood and bean salad
CONIGLIO RIPIENO CON VERDURA AL BURRO
Rabbit with greens sautéed in butter
INSALATA DI CAMPO CON FORMAGGIO
DI CAPRA
Green salad with goat cheese

Dolci

TORTA AL LIMONE
Lemon cake
TORTA DI FRUTTA FRESCA
Fresh fruit cake

BELLE DONNE

Via delle Belle Donne 16/red
Tel: 262609
Closed: Sat/Sun
Credit cards: No
Reservations: Advisable
Price: Moderate

FOLLOW THE BEAUTIFUL WOMEN

Without even a name over its door this small restaurant (30 seats) can best be found by spotting the cluster of people out front waiting to be seated. (For some reason beautiful women do show up here). Mario Bussi's place caters to the lunch crowd from nearby Via Tornabuoni and doesn't bother to open at all on weekends.

A counter piled high with a display of fruits and vegetables sets the tone. The ever-changing menu shows a light modern approach to Tuscan food; interesting salads and fish dishes lead the way. The pastas usually come with simple vegetable or fish sauces. The fresh poached salmon is accompanied by small boiled potatoes, red radishes and homemade mayonnaise.

The marble-topped tables are set with place mats of coarse butcher paper. The tin dispensers of olive oil are a nice touch. (If you'd like to have one for yourself try to buy one on the spot, otherwise you'll be sent to Bologna). The menu of the day is scrawled on a chalkboard in a corner of the room. If you find this inconvenient a waitress will be glad to recite the day's fare - in Italian, of course.

The excellent summertime fruit salad includes kiwi, cherries, strawberries and cantaloupe. Good simple homemade desserts are on offer. The wine list is short but some good bottles are available.

Antipasti

ALICI MARINATE
Marinated anchovies
INSALATA DI FUNGHI
Mushroom salad

Primi

FARFALLE CON GRANCHIO
Butterfly pasta with crabs
FUSILLI CON PUNTE DI ASPARAGI
Pasta with asparagus tips

Secondi

GALLINA BOLLITA
Boiled hen
SALMONE BOLLITO
Boiled salmon with mayonnaise
CARPACCIO DI MANZO
Thin slices of raw marinated beef

Dolci

MACEDONIA
Fresh fruit salad
PANNA COTTA
Rich cooked cream dessert

Coco Lezzone

Via del Parioncino 26/r
Tel: 287178
Closed: Sun/Tue eve; Aug.
Credit cards: No
Reservations: Not necessary
Price: High moderate

A SMALL TRATTORIA WITH CELEBRITY STATUS

With countless fine restaurants to choose from, where did La Marchesa Frescobaldi take Prince Charles to sample Tuscan cooking? Right here to the Smelly Cook, which is how the name translates. Smelly - but trustworthy and good - is the idea.

Coco Lezzone was famous some years ago when its two small rooms could seat only a handful of people at a time and dining here was like being a member of a family that had long since outgrown its house. Admittedly, it was a family that ate very well.

Now Coco has expanded into a normal sized room and everyone can enjoy the wonderful Tuscan dishes in a leisurely way. The pasta dishes with porcini mushrooms or truffles are justly praised if necessarily pricey. The meat dishes are excellent.

Have you ever eaten the famous Florentine dish la Trippa Fiorentina? That's tripe, a dish which can be found at over a dozen outdoor stands around the city the way tacos, hot dogs, falafels, etc. are sold elsewhere. If you want to give it a try, there's no better place than here at Coco Lezzone. Pale, tender, tasty, and attractively presented with a sprinkling of parmesan cheese, la trippa here is simply superb. If you've got a taste for it, that is.

Primi

PAPPA AL POMODORO
Tuscan tomato and bread soup
RIBOLLITA
Tuscan bread, bean and cabbage soup
FARFALLE CON FUNGHI PORCINI O TARTUFO BIANCO
Butterfly pasta with porcini mushrooms, or white truffles

Secondi

ARISTA DI MAIALE
Roast pork
TRIPPA ALLA FIORENTINA
Tripe in tomato sauce
BRACIOLE DI MANZO DELLA CASA
House steak chop with tomato sauce
INZIMINO
Squid with beet greens

Dolci

CASTAGNACCIO
Chestnut cake with pine nuts (available in winter)
BAVARESE
Mixed fruit or strawberries with chocolate

DONEY

Piazza Strozzi
Tel: 298206
Closed: Sun
Credit cards: All
Reservations: Advisable
Price: Lunch-Moderate/Dinner-Expensive

NEW DONEY IN THE PIAZZA

First opened by defeated Napoleonic campaigners in 1827 as a shop for French delicacies, Doney was for over a century the restaurant/salon of Florentine aristocrats. Well-heeled English visitors found the draw of Doney irresistible, as did most celebrities who visited Florence. The service was legendary, with waiters often outnumbering guests, the way the elite liked it. Over the years the old Doney became more streamlined, until it was finally forced to close in 1983.

Recently this great name in Florentine dining was revived by the designer Giorgio Armani whose Emporio shop is next door. Signor Armani has said that he likes to think of the resurrection of Doney as his present to Florence.

The new Doney offers something for everyone: it is a cafe and pasticceria, a place for cocktails and light lunches, and it is also a complete restaurant. There is outdoor seating under umbrellas in Piazza Strozzi. The revolutionary thing for Florence is that Doney stays open from ll a.m. straight through until midnight, and later. This is something to remember for anyone needing to eat during the downtime of the Italian riposo, or late at night.

As for the cuisine, it mirrors Giorgio Armani's fashion style: simple and elegant. Doney specializes in fish, always fresh.

Antipasti

FANTASIA DI GAMBERETTI DONEY
Vegetables and shrimp with oil and lemon
CARPACCIO DI MARE AL SALMONE
Slices of marinated salmon on a bed of rucola

Primi

CREPES ALLA MODA
Various crepes with bechamel sauce and tomato
PENNETTE ALLA CATALANA
Macaroni with fresh eggplant, bell peppers and zucchini
TAGLIERINI GRATINATI
Taglierini with bechamel and salmon sauce,
oven-browned

Secondi

TROTA BLEU CON SALSA MAIONESE
Blue trout with mayonnaise
ROMBO ALLA LIGURE
Turbot baked with herbs
PETTO DI POLLO ALL'INDIANA
Curried chicken breast
CHATEAUBRIANT
Chateaubriand beef fillet with bearnaise sauce

Dolci

CHEESECAKE
BAVARESE ALLA FRUTTA
Bavarian cream with fruit

Toula (Oliviero)

Rest. and American Bar
Via delle Terme 51/r
Tel: 287643
Closed: Sun/Mon lunch
Credit cards: Yes
Reservations: Advisable
Price: Expensive

A TOULA IN FLORENCE

The name Toula represents something highly unusual in Italian gastronomic life: a chain of luxury restaurants owned by a single financial group. However, *chain* is perhaps not the precise word since each Toula restaurant - in places like Torino, Milano and Rome as well as Tokyo - has its own identity.

Mario Benedetti, director of the Florence Toula which opened last year, explains. "We realize that every restaurant must have a life of its own starting with the individuality of the chef and expressing itself in the decor and in the particular style of service. The Toula group does not believe in stamping out clone restaurants".

To find its niche in Florence, Toula must above all win the hearts, and palettes, of Florentines. To that end, it does not offer dishes of the Tuscan countryside like the bread-thickened soups and long-cooked meats which are done to perfection by other specialty restaurants. Instead it concentrates on the classical Italian dishes like ravioli, and linguini with seafood sauces, while also offering standard international fare.

The goal is to provide the freshest and best ingredients possible, elegantly presented by professional waiters. Fresh fish is handled well here. (And if it isn't fresh, you can be sure it won't be served).

Antipasti

GRIGLIATA DI VERDURA "TOULA"
Grilled vegetables
BLINIS SALMONE
Salmon blini

Primi

RISOTTO ALLA MILANESE
Risotto with saffron
CRESPELLE AL FORMAGGIO BITTO E ERBETTE
CON NOCI GRATINATE
Crespelle with Bitto cheese herbs, and nuts

Secondi

BRANZINO IN SALSA DI ZUCCHINE,
MELANZANE, COZZE
Sea Bass with zucchini, eggplant and mussels
CHATEAUBRIAND CON SALSA BERNESE
Chateaubriand with bearnaise sauce

Dolci

SOUFFLE A GRAND MARNIER
DOLCI AL CARRELLO
Various cakes and puddings

I LATINI
Via dei Palchetti 6
Tel: 10916
Closed: Mon/Tues lunch and July 20
through August 8, and Christmas

From the queue of people in front of Latini's, you might think people were waiting to get into a smallish place instead of a sprawling restaurant of over 200 seats.

Latini's offers a special value in Florence: good solid fare at moderate prices in an atmosphere of bustle and high spirits. Expect to share wine and conversation with those around you since you will be seated, despite all the space, at communal tables.

Go early, or late, to avoid the queue. Or join the queue for a while if your appetite can bear it. It shouldn't take long since the turnover is fairly rapid.

CORSINI
Lungarno Corsini 4
Tel: 217706
Closed: Mon

This is a new luxury restaurant in a 14th century palazzo along the Arno.

MARIONE
Via della Spada 27/r
Tel: 214756
Closed: Wed

Two steps from Via Tornabuoni and full of working people for lunch. Good Florentine dishes at low prices.

ROSE'S CAFE
Via del Parione 26/r
Tel: 287090
Closed: Sun

By night Italian lads inspect the foreign girls at very close quarters. Limited menu for lunch and dinner.

SILVIO
Via del Parione 74/76/r
Tel: 214005
Closed: Sat/Sun

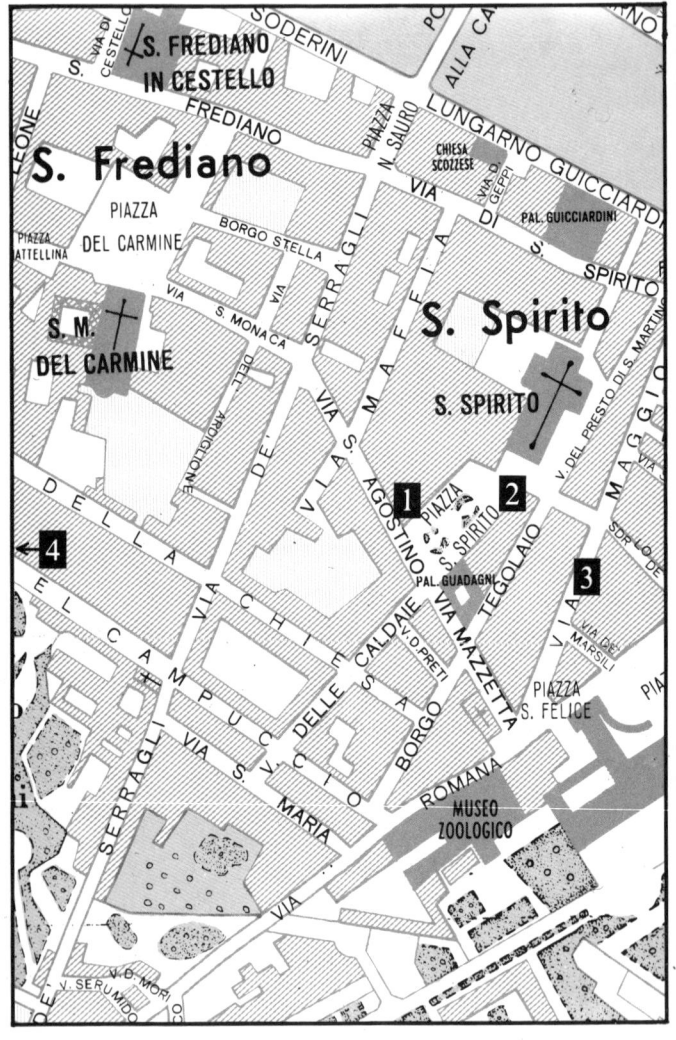

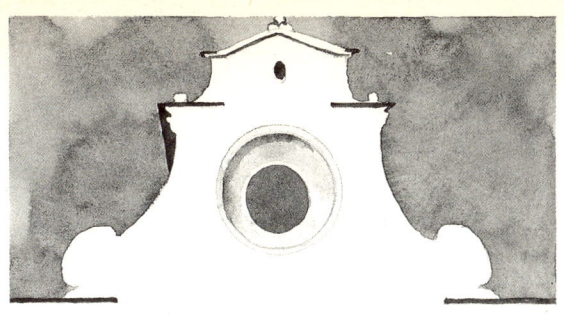

SANTO SPIRITO

Brunelleschi's Renaissance church. Most mornings farmers sell fruits and vegetables in the piazza. Michelangelo performed his notorious research on the human body in the morgue alongside the church.

1. ORESTE

2. BORGO ANTICO

3. LE QUATTRO STAGIONI

4. LA RUCOLA

5. I RADDI

ORESTE

Pizza Santo Spirito 16
Tel: 262383
(will take 2396009)
Closed: Wed
Credit cards: All
Reservations: Advisable
Price: Moderate

NEW KIDS ON THE PIAZZA

Just before going to print we noticed that Oreste had changed hands so we dutifully popped in to sniff things out. The consensus: This is a place to watch. The young owners come fresh from apprenticeships at two fine restaurants and bring to this venture enthusiasm, good will, and it would appear, plenty of talent. Outdoor seating in the piazza is a plus, and so are the reasonable prices.

The dishes we tasted were of high quality, even though it was opening night for the restaurant and some general confusion was evident.

Pastas are homemade, the tortellini filling tasty and satisfying. Meats are cooked with a light hand. The wine list is still short but the bottles available show that someone has a familiarity with quality wines. Allowing for inevitible growing pains, we think its safe to predict a bright future for Oreste.

Antipasti

CROSTINI AI FUNGHI
Toasted bread with mushroom spread

Primi

RISOTTO AROMATICO
Rice with fresh herbs
TORTELLINI NOCI E PROSCIUTTO
Tortellini with walnut and prosciutto filling
FARFALLE ALL'ORESTE CON PROSCIUTTO
AFFUMICATO E PISELLI
Butterfly pasta with smoked ham and peas

Secondi

CONIGLIO ALLA CACCIATORA
Rabbit cooked with in tomatoes and spices
SAMONE AL GUAZZETTO
Salmon with lemon, wine, and ginger
AGNELLO ALLA GRIGLIA
Grilled lamb

Dolci

TIRAMISU'
Cream, chocolate and cream cheese
PANNA COTTA
Cooked cream with cherry or strawberry sauce

BORGO ANTICO

(Trattoria/Pizzeria)
Piazza Santo Spirito 6
Tel: 210437
Closed: Sun/Mun lunch
Credit cards: No
Reservations: Advisable
Price: Moderate

PIZZA IN THE PIAZZA

Right on the beautiful piazza of Santo Spirito, the only piazza in the center of Florence graced with greenery and the shade of large leafy trees, this trattoria/pizzeria offers outdoor seating in the summertime. Inside the decor is rustic, all wood and brick, with the pizza oven in view.

The prices for the pizzas are a notch higher than usual, but here the pizzas are immense and good. (Florence is loaded with restaurants and trattorie but is somewhat thin on good pizzerias. See list before general index).

At Borgo Antico there are plenty of other good things on the menu as well. This is a popular place, so plan ahead. If it happens that you find yourselves waiting for a table at least you'll be able to pass the time in the piazza noted for having the most neighborhood spirit of any in Florence. Feel free to ask for a glass of wine while you wait.

Antipasti

RADICCHIO GRIGLIATO CON SCAMORZA
Grilled red chicory with buttery cheese
SPECK CON LE PERE
Cured ham with pears

Primi

FUSILLI PICCANTI CON TONNO E RUCOLA
Fusilli pasta with tuna and rucola lettuce
GNOCCHI AL RAGU DI SALSICCE
Gnocchi with sausage ragú

Secondi

STRACOTTO CON PATATE
Tuscan pot roast with potatoes
LE PIZZE
Wide selection of pizza

Dolci

DOLCI DELLA CASA
Sweets of the house

LE QUATTRO STAGIONI

Via Maggio 61
Tel: 218906
Closed: Sun/Sat in Summer and August
Credit cards: Amex/Diners/Mastercard
Reservations: Advisable
Price: Expensive

REFINED DINING IN ALL SEASONS

From the look of the outside of this trattoria there is no reason to expect anything very inspired inside. In this case however, the cover lies, because a visit to the Four Seasons weighs in as one of the most satisfying dining experiences in Florence.

Signor Piero Giannacci, owner and chef, has built a menu that ranges from Tuscan to classic Italian, and even brings in a French touch. The Insalata 'Caterina Medici' is the sort of thing rarely found in Florence, as is the chicken with gruyere and cognac. Risotto is a specialty here and is made with a variety of vegetables. If you see on the menu a risotto made with black ink squid in the Venetian style, jump at the chance to try it.

The common dishes of ravioli and tortelloni are uncommonly good. The fillings, made on the premises, are fresh and rich whether of porcini mushrooms or spinach/ricotta.

A dessert specialty is the custard with raisins and pine nuts. The wine list is not large, but contains some top Tuscan bottles. The simplicity of the decor is pleasing and the handpainted porcelain dishes speak of a refined, old world approach to dining.

Antipasti

INSALATA 'CATERINA MEDICI'
Capers, anchovies, cheese, walnuts, rughetta lettuce.
BARCHETTE ALLA FONTANA
Pastry boats filled with melted cheese.

Primi

LUNOTTO (RAVIOLI) DI CARCIOFI O TARTUFI
Half-moon ravioli with artichokes or truffles.
RISOTTO DI VERDURE DI STAGIONE
Risotto with vegetables of the season
GNOCCHI CON ZUCCA GIALLA
Gnocchi with yellow squash.

Secondi

INVOLTINI DI POLLO, PROSCIUTTO, GRUYERE, COGNAC
Chicken roll with prosciutto ham, gruyère, cognac
AGNELLO RIPIENO DI CARCIOFI
Lamb stuffed with artichoke, garlic, rosemary.
SCALOPPINE SAN MINIATO
Veal with milk cream and truffles.

Dolci

CREME CARAMEL
Custard with pine nuts and raisins

La Rucola

Via del Leone 50/red
(150 meters south of S.Spirito zone)
Tel: 224002
Closed: Sunday/every day lunch
Credit cards: Visa
Reservations: Advisable
Price: High moderate

A CHEF'S DOZEN

Luciano Ghinassi is clearly a whiz at the restaurant biz. He has been associated with numerous successes in Florence and his latest hit, La Rucola, is packing them in. Simple rustic decor inside, and a pleasant courtyard outside, are the settings for Signor Ghinassi's streamlined approach to fine eating.

The menu, which changes often, bypasses antipasti altogether and offers only a dozen dishes: six firsts and six main courses. You are expected to order one of each. The second course comes with two vegetables. As if to spare you even a moment's distraction from mundane matters, all first courses cost the same, just as the main courses all share a single price.

Technical concerns aside, La Rucola falls into the category of Tuscan restaurants that re-create interesting old recipes from the countryside while feeling free to invent and improvise. The preparation and presentation of these dishes are impeccable. Always on the menu are some authentic alternatives to pasta dishes, inspired from the days when Tuscans didn't eat much pasta. The *gnocchi* and *malfatti* found here require a good deal of artistry. Meats are handled with a knowing touch, often coming with interesting sauces.

Another specialty is fresh fish baked with herbs in a pouch of foil paper. This is an aromatic and healthful way to cook fish which we should all learn.

Primi

MALFATTI AI FIORI DI ZUCCA
Small dumplings of ricotta cheese and zucchini flowers
SFOGLIATA AL PREZZEMOLO E NOCI
Flakey pastry filled with ricotta, parsley and walnuts
RISOTTO ALLA BIETOLA E STRACCHINO
Risotto with beet greens and stracchino cheese

Secondi

CARRE' DI VITELLA AL CEDRO
Veal chop in citron sauce
CONIGLIO RIPIENO CON FUNGHI PORCINI
Rabbit meat roll with porcini mushrooms
ROSETTA DI VITELLA AL CURRY CON RISO PILAF
Curried veal roll with rice pilaf
TRANCIO DI PESCE SPADA AL CARTOCCIO
Swordfish baked in a pouch

Dolci

PANNA COTTA CON LAMPONI
Cooked cream with raspberry sauce
BAVARESE AL CIOCCOLATO
Bavarian cream pudding with chocolate sauce

I Raddi

Via d'Ardiglione 47/r
Tel: 211072
Closed: Sun/Month of August
Credit cards: Amex
Reservations: Advisable
Price: Moderate

WHERE THE LOCALS ARE

Here is a good family-run trattoria somewhat off-the-beaten-track, a 'find' of the sort that a reviewer almost regrets exposing. The decor is rustic. Immense beams support a wooden ceiling, the furniture is country style and the appropriate terra-cotta tiles are underfoot.

As for the food, the crostini are as they ought to be, the various spreads laid on at the last moment on freshly toasted bread. The pastas are fresh and the ragu sauces are cooked scrupulously long. The Taglierini Ardiglione, named after the street, is an example: the sausage, tomatoes and herbs having comuned so long in the pan together as to have totally merged their personalities into one potent sauce.

The long-cooked beef dish Peposo shares the same virtues and is as peppery as the name implies. The dish is from the 14th century and is supposed to have been a favorite of Brunelleschi the architect. (You can bet he knew a thing or two about long-cooked projects. That famous egg he placed on top of the cathedral took over 80 years to complete).

I Raddi is sparsely visited at lunchtime but has a good local following in the evening. The wine list contains some excellent Tuscan reds and is being built up methodically.

Antipasti

MISTO TOSCANO
Assorted paté and sliced meats
SOTT'OLIO CASALINGHI
Assorted vegetables in oil

Primi

TAGLIERINI ARDIGLIONE
Fresh pasta with tomato, sausage and herbs
TAGLIERINI CON ERBETTE
Fresh pasta with a mix of 16 fresh herbs

Secondi

PEPOSO ALLA FORNACINA
Beef spezzatino with pepper, garlic, red wine and tomato
SCOTTIGLIA
Stew of pigeon, hen, duck, dove, rabbit and lamb
BUDELLINA
Milk fed veal sweetbread
BISTECCA ALLA FIORENTINA
Florentine beefsteak

Dolci

PANNACOTTA
Cooked cream
PINOLATA
Pine nut torte

Cantinone del Gallo Nero
Via Santo Spirito 6/red
Tel: 218898
Closed: Mon

One problem in Florence these days is finding a relatively inexpensive bite to eat someplace where you're permitted to actually sit down. (If you've never been stung before, be warned that most cafes and snack bars in the center of Florence demand a 100% surcharge if you sit at one of their tables to do your snacking).

The Cantinone is perhaps your best bet in the area for a quick, tasty inexpensive lunch or snack. Down here in the cellars the staple dishes are ribollita, sausage and beans, and various crostoni, which are large slices of bread toasted in the oven with pizza-like toppings. The bread used is the authentic Tuscan type: no salt, naturally leavened, baked in a woodburning oven. The toppings include cheese, prosciutto, red and yellow peppers, artichokes, and of course tomatoes.

In summer the Cantinone also serves Panzanella, a cold salad made of bread, onion, tomatoes, cucumbers and basil. Delicious. You sit at communal tables. The only beverages to choose from are wine (red, white, or rosé) or mineral water. No soft drinks.

Trattoria Casalinga
Via del Michelozzi 9/red
Tel: 218624
Closed: Sunday

Probably the cheapest place in town. Nothing at all wrong with the food. Despite the low prices they'll even give you half portions of some meat dishes.

Trattoria San Agostino
Via San Agostini 23
Tel 210208
Closed: Sun eve/Mon

Contains immense wine cellar containing rather too many old wines. Be sure your Burton Anderson guide to Italian wines gives the green light before trying anything from a previous generation.

Trattoria Angiolino
Via Santo Spirito 36
Tel: 298976
Closed: Mon

Angiolino seems to be living in a time warp. On and on it goes, resisting change and serving up dependable Tuscan meals. Some of the regulars here look positively dug in, as if acutely aware of occupying a private haven from the changing world outside.

In winter, when the large iron stove in the center of the room glows with heat, Angiolino has charm. The waiters, however, are decidedly grumpy.

Antica Cantina Capponi
Borgo San Frediano 26/red
Tel: 292130
Closed: Tues

Solid menu in a small cellar.

Trattoria Del Carmine
Piazza del Carmine 18
Tel: 218601
Closed: Sunday

Diladdarno
Via Serragli 108/ red
Tel: 225001
Closed: Monday

Nello
Borgo Tegolaio 21
Tel: 218511
Closed: Mon/Tue lunch

OUTSIDE FLORENCE

1. La Graziella

2. Capannina Di Sante

3. Omero

4. Pane e Vino

5. Centanni

La Graziella

(Maiano, 4 km north of Florence)
Tel. 599963
End of short Maiano road.
Day Closed: Monday
Credit cards: Visa, Mastercharge
Reservations: Advisable
Price: Moderate

SARDINIAN SPECIALITIES IN THE FLORENTINE HILLS

This new trattoria offers excellent food at a great price as well as plenty of outdoor seating under trees on a hillside below Fiesole.

Ugo Salis, the driving force behind this refreshing trattoria, came to Florence from Sardinia over 20 years ago. He met a Scottish girl from Inverness, albeit of Italian descent, married and began his career in the restaurant business. After years of cooking for top Florentine trattorie and a brief stint cooking in Inverness (his wife cried for Florence and back they came) he has finally achieved his dream: to cook Sardinian dishes in his own restaurant.

A meal at La Graziella begins with *pane carasau*, a paper thin fried bread. The appetizers are mainland: tomato and oregano on toast, eggplant, crostini. A shell-like pasta common in Sardinia is called mallureddus and comes with a sausage ragu sauce. The homemade tortelloni are a delicacy not to be found anywhere else in Florence. The filling is made from fresh sheep cheese that has sat out for 24 hours to take on the slightest edge of fermentation. The veal ragú sauce is first rate.

Though Sardinia is of course an island, the Sardinians have taken to the sea only recently. For millenia they have been shepherds and so their specialities are grilled and roasted meats. Porcetta is young roasted milk-fed pork not to be confused with porchetta (the *c* alone is soft, with an *h* it becomes hard) which is mature pork and a dish of another color. The grilled lamb comes as little steaks cut from the leg in the Sardinian style. Usually, in Lazio and

Tuscany lamb is served either as a classic leg or small rib chops.

La Graziella is fortunate to receive its meat, fresh ricotta and sheep cheeses from Sardinian shepherd friends who live in the nearby hills.

Ugo Salis is a hardworker who shakes his head in disbelief at the tourist restaurants that dare serve ragu sauces cooked barely an hour. He would never dream of serving a ragú cooked less than 6 hours. He's right. You can taste the difference.

The wine list is short but includes the Chiantis, including Riservas, that you'll need to accompany the ragus and the roasted meats. If you want to go all the way with the taste of Sardinia try Abbaia, a fine red not as strong as some of the other notorious reds from the sun-drenched island.

Ugo's only complaint is that the Trattoria Le Cave di Maiano, which is a bare 100 meters down the road and has been in all the guidebooks for a decade, confuses many customers trying to find his establishment. "Even my friends don't always make it all the way up the hill, stopping at Le Cave by mistake".

We should enjoy La Graziella while we can. Ugo Salis has one more dream to achieve, a return to Sardinia where his heart has always remained.

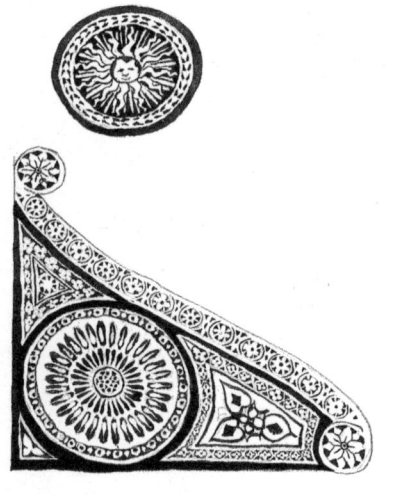

Antipasti

PANE CARASAU
Paper thin bread

Primi

SPAGHETTI ALLA BOTTARGA
Spaghetti with fish roe
MALLUREDDUS ALLA SARDA
Shell-like pasta with sausage ragú
TORTELLONI DELLA CASA
Tortelloni with pecorino cheese, potato, orange peel

Secondi

MAIALINI DI LATTE ALLA SARDA
Roasted milk-fed pork
CARPACCIO DI BOTTARGA
Slices from fish roe loaf
AGNELLO GRIGLIATO ALLA SARDA
Grilled lamb

Dolci

TIRAMISU' CON FICHI E NOCI
Tiramisù with figs and walnuts
SEBADAS
Pastry with pecorino cheese and honey

CAPANNINA DI SANTE

At Ponte da Verrazzano and Piazza Ravenna
Tel: 688345 - (2.5 km east of P. Vecchio)
Closed: Sun/mon lunch/Aug
Credit card: All
Reservations: Advisable
Price: Expensive

DELICIOUS FRESH FISH

Sante Collesano is a Sicilian who insists that he owes his place today as one of Florence's most respected restaurateurs to the lessons he learned in London years ago preparing Tuscan dishes. There he grasped the great value of specialization: choose one thing and do it well.

Since he had once been a fisherman Sante figured that the one thing he knew about was fish. One of the many ways in which curly-haired, still boyish Sante charms is with his honesty. "I thought I knew about fish. But I didn't really. In those early years my customers and I learned together".

According to Sante, honesty is the most important attribute for anyone in the fish game. "I wanted to establish total trust between me and my customers". Today most of his customers don't bother to look at the menu, they just say "bring it on", knowing that Sante will serve them what's freshest and best. Every other day Sante travels to the fish market in Marcignana, some 50 kilometers from Florence, or to the seaside market of Follonica, to personally choose the best catches.

His present restaurant is on the south bank of the Arno some 2500 meters upstream from the Ponte Vecchio. There is additional seating outdoors under a roof. It's all fish, beginning with a variety of hot and cold appetizers. Don't pass up the Spaghetti di mare under the mistaken assumption that it will be just another spaghetti dish with a few clams thrown in. When the plate is laid before you, you may have some trouble finding the pasta, hidden as it is beneath a colorful coral reef of clams, mussels and prawns.

For the main course choose between a plate of scampi and lobster, or a whole fish.

Antipasti

PESCE MARINATO
Marinated fish
COZZE E GAMBERI MARINARA
Mussels and shrimps with garlic

Primi

SPAGHETTI DI MARE
Spaghetti with seafood
FETTUCCINE ALL'ARAGOSTA
Fettuccini with lobster

Secondi

SCAMPI
Prawns
ARAGOSTA
Lobster
BRANZINO
Sea bass

Dolci

BAVARESE AL LIMONE
Lemon cream pudding

OMERO

Via Pian dei Giullari 11/r
Tel. 220053 - (3 km south of Florence)
Closed: Tues/August
Credit cards: Amex/Mastercard
Reservations: Necessary
Price: High moderate

COUNTRY TRATTORIA NEAR FLORENCE

It's hard to beat this location in the hills overlooking Florence. For a special evening you'll want a table by the windows, so book ahead and ask for a *tavola con panorama*. Omero is located just a short ride from Florence on a winding road lined with villas. Across the road from Omero is where Galileo Galilei lived in exile.

Omero is a country style trattoria which relies on the tried and true Florentine specialities. All the Florentine bread dishes are here, from garlic bread (fettunta) to the summer salad panzanella. Meats, chicken and rabbit are either grilled over a charcoal fire or deep fried in olive oil. The *Bistecca alla Fiorentina,* charcoal grilled and served rare, is naturally at the heart of the menu. Artichokes come fried with or without batter. The best cheeses are usually the Tuscan sheep cheeses, aged or fresh, which go so well with wine. The wine list here includes just about every fine Tuscan red available.

In true country style the entrance to the trattoria is occupied by a food shop specializing in cured meats and cheeses. Before leaving, you'd do well to stock up.

Antipasti

CROSTINI TOSCANI
Mixed Tuscan crostini
SALUMI MISTI
Prosciutto and salame

Primi

RIBOLLITA
Thick vegetable and bread suop
RAVIOLI RICOTTA E SPINACI
Ricotta and spinach filled ravioli
PAPPARDELLE ALLA LEPRE
Pappardelle pasta with rabbit sauce

Secondi

BISTECCA ALLA FIORENTINA
Florentine Beefsteak
FRITTO MISTO
Deep fried chicken and rabbit
INZIMINO
Beet greens and squid

Dolci

MERINGA
Meringue

PANE E VINO

Via Poggio Bracciolini 48
Piazza Gavinana - (2.5 km east of P. Vecchio)
Tel. 683746
Closed: Sunday, Holidays
(open evenings only)
Credit cards: All
Price: High moderate

HOMAGE TO THE GOOD GRAPE

If you enjoy tasting a series of fine wines accompanied by refined side dishes, then you will definitely find it worth the slight inconvenience of getting yourself to Piazza Gavinana, two kilometers up river. (Bus no. 23 leaves from the Station and the Duomo. Ask to be let out at P. Gavinana. The last return bus passes at 12.22 a.m.)

The brothers Gilberto and Ubaldo Pierazzuoli, who come from the Casentino area near Arezzo, are a perfect example of how it can sometimes happen that people who are simply following their interests, without any plan, can drift into the right careers. Just over a decade ago the brothers began to gather with friends to "talk about" fine wines. Those sessions blossomed and continue today at the site of their *Enoteca* (wine shop) and restaurant, Pane e Vino.

The food here is light, interesting and carefully prepared. Please note, however, that the dishes are designed to play supporting roles to the wines. Paté, quiche, carpaccio, and cheese dishes make up the heart of the menu. The paté are light Tuscan versions using chicken and calf livers, or fine-quality cooked ham. Standard pasta and meat dishes are not served here.

In Florence, probably only Giorgio Pinchiorri (p. 62) keeps his ears to the ground for viticultural news with the ardor shown by the Pierazzuoli brothers. Some 700 diverse labels pass through the shop yearly. You may not find here all the big names from our wine list because the Pierazzuoli prefer to use their limited space to stock rare and unusual wines. Not many foreign visitors make their way to Pane e Vino. If you are not an Italian speaker, don't expect the conversation to get very far. But if you let it be known that you have come to taste wines (*per assaggiare i vini*) you will be taken well in hand.

INSALATA DI FUNGHI
Mushroom salad

MOUSSE DI FEGATO O PROSCIUTTO O ARINGHE CON PISTACCHI
Mousse of calf and chicken livers or fine ham or herring

CROSTONI DI FEGATO O FUNGHI
Crostone with liver or porcini mushrooms

CROSTINI DI CAVOLO NERO
Crostini with black cabbage

MAIALE CON GINGER
Pork with ginger

SPINACI LORRAINE
Spinach Lorraine

BAVARESE DI PERA CON SALSA DI FRAGOLE
Pear and cream pudding with strawberries

CENTANNI

Via Centanni 7
Bagno a Ripoli
(7km east of Florence)
Tel: 630122
Closed: Sat/Sun/August
Credit cards: All
Reservation: Advisable
Price: Expensive

GOURMETS IN THE NEARBY COUNTRYSIDE

If you were thinking of taking time out for a first-class meal in a beautiful country setting near Florence, Centanni might be exactly the place. (Bus no. 23 from the train station will take you, in about 20 minutes, to within a few hundred yards of the restaurant. Buses stop running around midnight).

Dine either on a large terrace, or inside the restaurant from where the views are just as good or better, thanks to the large windows which give on to a perfect scene of Tuscan hills. Centanni is strictly a family affair in which everyone has his or her own turf to patrol. Luciano is the pastry chef, Silvano the sommelier, and Silvia makes the ravioli of the house herself according to a special recipe.

Along with most of the standard Tuscan starters, Centanni offers a light plate of rucola lettuce, parmesean cheese and thin sliced zucchini. A specialty is the ravioli filled with pigeon meat, breadcrumbs, cheese and spices. This dish has a wonderful flavor and texture, and convincingly argues for the excellence of properly raised pigeon, in this case, bred locally.

Meat and fish dishes are top-notch. This is another good opportunity for a thick rare Florentine beefsteak. The wine list is replete with superb Tuscan red wines which match up well with steak.

For a special treat, ask if any fresh goat cheeses are on hand from the Antinori farms. Luciano suggests you have them with a specialty wine by Monsanto called Botritis. This wine is made of white grapes left on the vines well into November and then aged for years. The result is a strong and peculiar flavour that seems just the thing as long as the goat cheese is still around, less so on its own.

Antipasti

RUCOLA, PARMIGIANO E ZUCCHINE
Salad of rucola parmesean and zucchini

Primi

CAPPELLETTI DI PICCIONE
Ravioli with pigeon stuffing
TAGLIATELLE DI MELANZANE E ZUCCHINE
Tagliatelle with eggplant and zucchini
RAVIOLI SPINACI E RICOTTA
Ravioli of ricotta and spinach

Secondi

ANATRA IN UMIDO CON SEDANI
Duck stewed in the oven with celery
STRACOTTO DEL '600
Pot roast with almonds, pine nuts, raisins and red wine
IL GRAN PEZZO
Standing rib roast

Dolci

PESCHE COTTE CON ZABAIONE CALDO
Cooked peaches with hot zabaione
CREPES CON PERE, MANDORLE, PINOLI, CIOCCO-
LATO CALDO
Crepes, with pear, almonds, pine nuts and chocolate

IL BARONE
Via Romano 123/r
Tel: 220585
Closed: Sun

Well-established gourmet spot which operates somewhat like a museum, offering weekly gastronomic theme exhibitions. Recent themes have been vegetarian, Colombian, rustic country, and dishes with aquavit.

VECCHIA BETTOLA
Viale L. Ariosto 34
Tel: 224158
Closed: Sun/Mon

Very popular and good trattoria.

LE CAVE DI MAIANO
Via delle Cave 16
Maiano (Fiesole)
Tel: 59133
Closed: Thurs/Sun evening

A Florentine institution for years

TRATTORIA VITTORIA (FISH)
Via della Fonderia 52/r
Tel: 225657
Closed: Wed

ANTICO CRESPINO
Largi Fermi 15
Tel: 221158
Closed: Wed

LA LOGGIA
Piazzale Michelangelo 1
Tel: 287032
Closed: Wed

LO STRETTOIO
Via Serpiolle 7
Tel: 403044
Closed: Sun/Mon

A SELECTION OF TUSCAN RESTAURANTS

Prato
TRATTORIA BRUNO
Via Verdi 12
Prato - (20 km NW of Florence)
Tel: 0574.23810
Closed: Thur eve/Sun/August
Price: High moderate

San Casciano
L'ANTICA POSTA
Piazza Zannoni 1
San Casciano in Val di Pesa - (18 km S of Florence)
Tel: 055.820116
Closed: Mon/Aug
Price: Expensive

Greve
DA VERRAZZANO
Piazza Matteotti 28
Greve - (27 km S of Florence)
Tel: 853189
Closed: Sun eve/Mon
Price: Moderate

Siena
RISTORANTE MEDIO EVO
Via dei Rossi 40
Siena - (70 km S of Florence)
Tel: 0577.280315
Closed: Thur
Price: Expensive

Il Pozzo
Piazza Roma
Monteriggioni (SI) - (55 km S of Florence)
Tel: 0577.304127
Closed: Sun eve. and all Mon
Price: High moderate

San Gimignano
Le Terrazze
Piazza della Cisterna 24
San Gimignano - (57 km S of Florence)
Tel: 0577.240328
Closed: Tue/Wed lunch
Price: High moderate

Cerbaia
La Tenda Rossa
Piazza del Monumento 9-14
Cerbaia - (20 km SW of Florence)
Tel: 055.826132
Closed: Wed
Price: Expensive

Arezzo
Buca San Francesco
Via San Francesco 1
Arezzo - (80 km SE of Florence)
Tel: 0575.23271
Closed:
Price: Moderate

San Vincenzo
Gambero Rosso
Piazza della Vittoria 13
San Vincenzo - (130 km SW of Florence)
Tel: 0565.701021
Closed: Tue/Nov
Price: Expensive

Lucca

DA GIULIO
Via S.Tommaso 29 «Pelleria» - (zone Porta S.Donato)
Lucca - (75 km W of Florence)
Tel: 0583.55948
Closed: Sun/Mon/August
Price: High moderate

LA MORA
Via Sesto da Moriano 1748
Ponte a Moriano - (8 km N of Lucca)
Tel: 0583.57109
Closed: Wed eve/Thur
Price: Moderate

Pisa

AL RISTORO DEI VECCHI MACELLI
Via Volturno 49
Pisa - (95 km W of Florence)
Tel: 050.20424
Closed: Sun/Wed/August
Price: Moderate

Pietrasanta - Viareggio
Forte dei Marmi

IL BAFFARDELLO
Via Ficalucci 46
Marina di Pietrasanta (LU - 105 km W of Florece)
Tel: 0584.21034
Closed: Thur
Price: High moderate

DA CLARA
Via Aurelia 289
Lido di Camaiore (LU - 5 km N of Viareggio)
Tel: 0584.904520
Closed: Mon
Price: Moderate

Castello di Uzzano

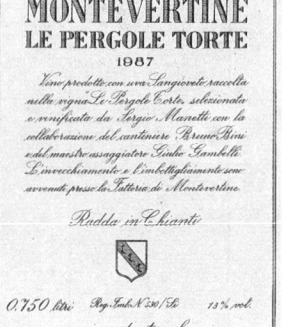

THE WINES OF TUSCANY

These are great days for Tuscan wine. The promise of the early 1970's, when big money and viticulture expertise moved into Tuscany in a serious way, has been superbly realized. During the past two decades winemaking in the region has been radically updated and the overhaul has, well, borne some wonderful fruit. What's more, Tuscany has been blessed with a string of excellent vintages from 1985 through 1988. The best bottles are only now appearing in wine shops after several years of cellar ageing.

Sangiovese

The king of Tuscan grapes is Sangiovese. Virtually all the top red wines of the region, including Chianti, Brunello di Montalcino, Vino Nobile di Montepulciano and Carmignano are made predominantly of Sangiovese, or Sangiovese clones. Other local varieties have always been used in supporting roles to round out wines whose essential characters are defined by Sangiovese.

The lure of the marketplace has inspired Tuscan producers to plant new vineyards with internationally known varieties such as Cabernet Sauvignon and Cabernet Franc, Merlot, Pinot Noir and Chardonnay. Athough most of these vines appear to flourish in Tuscan soil - Cabernet Sauvignon especially has proved an enormous success here both alone and in blends with Sangiovese - the feeling among most Italian wine people is that Sangiovese will survive the current infatuation with 'foreign' varieties and will remain the flavor of Tuscany.

Chianti

A name known around the world, Chianti is too often associated with a light red wine, cheap and cheerful, flowing from strawcovered flasks (*fiaschi*) wherever Italian food is found.

Admittedly, Chianti was until recently overproduced, usually with little regard for quality. Too often the weak or rough liquid under the Chianti label wasn't worth the little we were asked to pay for it. But how things have changed! And quickly, too, considering the inherent slowness of the wine making process. In the last ten years Chianti producers have reduced their yields by half in an effort to improve quality. The turnaround has amazed critics and has been described as no less than a revolution. We may regret the passing of the picturesque flasks but we can only applaud that more fine wine, and often great wine, is being bottled under the name of Chianti than ever before.

The revolution in Tuscan winemaking hasn't been limited to Chianti. All wines in the region have benefitted from new technology and the worldwide trends favoring fine wines.

Chianti Consortia

The two major consortia which look after the interests of Chianti wines are Gallo Nero (Black Rooster) for the Chianti Classico zone and Putto (Cherub) for all the other Chianti zones. Chianti under one of these two labels is usually a safe bet. It should be stressed that a good deal of creative nonconformity exists among Chianti producers. As a result some of the very best wines coming from the Chianti zones do not carry a consortium label. Other producers have gone so far as to snub the name Chianti altogether, making do with the only other label the law allows: *vino da tavola*, or table wine.

The Wine Laws

The Italian wine laws known as DOC, which controls name and origin, came into effect in the early 1960's at a time when some sort of regulation was desperately needed to bring a degree of order to the total disarray within the Italian wine scene.

Although the DOC laws have been severely criticized ("too lenient regarding maximum yields, too rigid in their insistence on long ageing in wood and on certain outmoded formulas for well-established wines"), the consensus over the years is that these imperfect laws have been vastly preferable to none at all. A structure was imposed on the industry giving it something to work with, and against. The mere attempt at organization gave the industry a tremendous boost in morale. One unintended result of the DOC laws was that creative winemakers were confronted with clear guidelines to analyze, dispute and rebel against. The new directions taken by certain free-spirited producers have been vital to the development of Tuscan wines.

The DOC status is sometimes expanded to DOCG. The G stands for Guaranteed, meaning that the wine has been approved by a tasting board.

Super Vino da Tavola

Vino da tavola means ordinary table wine. At least, that is the literal meaning. As a result of certain DOC regulations which forced restive producers outside the law, the term has come to mean something entirely different. When strongwilled Tuscan winemakers decided to defy DOC stipulations, whether concerning the varieties allowed in a wine or the amount of ageing required, they could no longer use a DOC appellation for their renegade wines. Furthermore, they were obliged to label their individualistic creations with the humble title of *Vino da Tavola*. This turned out to be a monumental blunder on the part of the lawmakers.

Led by Sassicaia (see p.178), and soon followed by Antinori's Tignanello and a spate of other self-styled wines, *Vino da Tavola* has become nothing less than the glamour category. Anything but ordinary, these super table wines represent the cream of Tuscan production. They have won international acclaim and sell for prices previously unheard of for Tuscan wines (with the exception of the legendary Brunello of Biondi Santi).

THE WINE LIST

RED WINES

Vintages 80 81 82 83 85 86 87 88

Because of all the variables involved in winemaking, most notably diverse microclimates, it is impossible to know how individual producers fared in a particular year without actually tasting each of their wines. Generally speaking, all vintages of the 1980's were good to excellent except for the lean years of 1984 and 1989. The banner years of '82 and '85 yielded what have been hailed as super vintages, with '86 and '88 not far behind.

CHIANTI

Traditionally Chianti has been a light fruity wine made for early consumption. The austerity of its black grapes, mostly Sangiovese, was always tempered by a hefty addition of white grapes. This custom was codified as the official Chianti formula by Baron Ricasoli back in the last century. Now the trend is definitely toward Chianti wines with greater body, complexity and ageing capacity. The practice of adding white grapes to a Chianti meant to be aged is currently condemned by most producers. Nevertheless, the official Chianti formula still calls for a small percentage of white varieties.

Because of varying terrains and microclimates, as well as the differing styles of vinification within the Chianti zones, there is not simply one Chianti wine, but a great many. Someday Chianti vineyards will doubtless be classified by *crus*, in the manner of the famous French vineyards.

There are seven designated regions which are entitled to use the name Chianti. The zones near Florence are Colli Fiorentini, Chianti Classico, Rufina and Montalbano. The other three are Colli Senesi, Colli Aretini, and Colline Pisane in the hills around Siena, Arezzo and Pisa.

Only three of these regions are said to adhere strictly to the laws that govern their production. They are Chianti

Classico, Chianti Rufina, and Chianti Colli Fiorentini. The other zones may produce fine wine but their output is inconsistent and we shouldn't yet pay much attention to their claims of controls and guarantees.

CHIANTI CLASSICO

Chianti Classico is made from grapes grown in the Chianti heartland between Florence and Siena. Wine from this region is not necessarily better than other Chianti. However, the Gallo Nero consortium which monitors production methods of Chianti Classico has by and large done an excellent job. The only other region to reach such high overall standards is that of Rufina.

Chianti Classico is usually at its peak after 2-5 years.

RISERVA

The term Riserva refers to wines made specifically to be aged. Since Chianti is by nature an austere wine that benefits enormously from ageing, the Riservas are superior to normal Chianti.

The best Chianti Riservas tend to come from the Chianti Classico and Rufina zones and are at their peak between 4-8 years, though some can go on much longer.

Chianti is served with most regional dishes. With the renowned Florentine beefsteak a Chianti Riserva or another of the big Tuscan reds is recommended.

Some top producers:

CHIANTI CLASSICO

Badia a Coltibuono
Berardenga
Capannelle Castellare
Castell'in Villa
Castello di Fonterutoli
Castello di Querceto
Castello di San Polo in Rosso
Castello di Uzzano
Castello di Volpaia
Castello Vicchiomaggio
Fontodi
Fossi
Isole e Olena
Lilliano
Monsanto
Montagliari
Monte Vertine
Nozzole
Pagliarese
Podere Il Palazzino
Podere Marcellina
Poggio al Sole
Poggio Rosso
Riecine
Riserva Ducale (Ruffino)
Rocca delle Macie
San Felice
Santa Cristina-Antinori
Savignola Paolina
Ser Niccolo
Terrarossa-Melini
Vecchie Terre di Montefili
Vignamaggio
Vignavecchia
Villa Antinori
Billa Banfi
Villa Rosa
Vistarenni

CHIANTI RUFINA

Castello di Nipozzano-Frescobaldi
Montesodi-Frescobaldi
Poggio a Remole-Frescobaldi
Spalletti
Poggio Reale
Selvapiana
Villa di Ponte
Villa di Vetrice

CHIANTI COLLI FIORENTINI

Castello di Poppiano
Fattoria dell'Ugo
Fattoria Pagnana
Fattoria il Corno
La Querce
Montegufoni
Tenuta il Monte
Torre a Decima

CHIANTI COLLINE SENESI

Avignonese
Castelpugna
Riccardo Falchini
Fattoria del Cerro
Fattoria Il Paradiso
La Muraglia
Poliziano
Villa Cusona (Guicciardini Strozzi)

CHIANTI MONTALBANO

Bibbiani
Fattoria di Artimino
Fattoria di Bacchereto
Fattoria Il Poggiolo
Tenuta di Capezzana

CHIANTI COLLI ARETINI

Monte Petrognano
Villa Cilnia
Villa la Selva

CARMIGNANO

The Grand Duchy of Tuscany first recognized this wine region (west of Florence) as one of controlled name and origin back in 1716. Carmignano is best known for its noble reds which are smooth and dry, with intriguing complexity and a flowery bouquet. Carmignano now includes from 5-10% Cabernet which provides that touch of Bordeaux elegance. Carmignano reds are the most consistent of any wines in Tuscany because they are subjected to tastings by experts before being approved. Of particular excellence is the Camignano Riserva by Count Ugo Contini Bonacossi of Villa Capezzana.

Fattoria Ambra
Fattoria di Artimino
Fattoria di Bacchereto
Fattoria di Calavria
Fattoria il Poggiolo
Fattoria Le Farnete
Fattoria Lo Locco
Villa Capezzana
Villa di Trefiano

POMINO

Pomino is a new DOC appellation for red, white and vin santo wines from the Rufina area which is one of the oldest recognized zones in Tuscany. The Pomino rosso is based on Sangiovese with the addition of Canaiolo, Cabernet, and Merlot. It is a well-balanced, harmonious wine capable of ageing. The bianco is based on Pinot Bianco and Chardonnay and is a dry dinner wine.

Marchesi de' Frescobaldi

BRUNELLO DI MONTALCINO

Made from the Brunello grape (a clone of Sangiovese) these reds can be among the greatest in Italy. Brunello is a large well-structured wine known for its long life and wonderfully complex bouquet and flavor. The most famous and expensive Brunello is made by Biondi-Santi which has been making the wine for over a hundred years and whose cellars still contain some of the original bottles.

Many new producers have entered the field in recent years - the number is now over 100 - and there is confusion as to what actually constitutes a Brunello. Many feel that the DOCG requirement to age Brunello 3 1/2 years in wooden casks is excessive. Some new producers are strongly challenging the supremacy of the traditional makers.

Altesino
Biondi-Santi (Il Greppo)
Camigliano
Case Basse
Castelgiocondo
Cerbaiona
Fattoria dei Barbi
La Chiesa di Santa Restituta
La Casa - Caparzo
La Gerla
Lisini
Poggio Antico
Tenuta Caparzo
Tenuta Il Poggione
Villa Banfi

VINO NOBILE DI MONTEPULCIANO

This wine of the grand name and legendary fame (the 17th century poet Francesco Redi called it "the king of all wines") has been causing the brows of wine connoisseurs to furrow with concern. It simply hasn't been living up to its billing. Many of the old producers of Vino Nobile appear to have been resting on their laurels. However, now that the wine revolution in Italy has truly taken hold, the producers of Vino Nobile seem to be waking up and heeding the call.

Certainly the best Vino Nobile can hold its own in any company, as demonstrated by the refined wines of Avignonesi and De Ferrari Corradi. A top Vino Nobile closely resembles a well-made Chianti Riserva.

Avignonesi
Fratelli Bologna Bonsignori
Buracchi
Cantine Baiocchi
Cantine Riunite Mario Contucci
Carletti della Giovampaola
De Ferrari Corradi
Fassati
Fattoria Casalte
Fattoria di Fognano
Tenuta Trerose
Tenuta Valdipiatta

ROSSO DI MONTALCINO

This is a new appellation for Brunello-like wines which for some reason or another (e. g. insufficient ageing in wood) cannot legally call themselves Brunello. Though not as complex as Brunello, these wines can be excellent - vigorous and full-bodied. Rosso di Montalcino often gives great value for money.

Altesino
Camigliano
Case Basse
Castelgiocondo
Centine - Villa Banfi
La Chiesa di Santa Restituta
La Casa - Caparzo
La Gerla
Lisini
Poggio Antico
Tenuta Caparzo

Tenuta Il Poggione
Val di Suga
Villa Nicola-Iacocca

SUPER VINI DA TAVOLA

As explained above, "ordinary table wines" can be among the finest in Italy and the most expensive. They do not have DOC status and do not seek it. By now the super wines of this category have a prestige of their own. Most of these new-style wines are aged in small barrels of Slavonic or French oak. Sangiovese and Cabernet Sauvignon grapes share top billing, but other red wine varieties like Mammolo, Canaiolo, and Merlot also figure. (Brunello, Sangioveto, and Prugnolo all belong to the Sangiovese family). In the list that follows the first named grape variety predominates.

WINE	PRODUCER	GRAPES
Alto Altese	Altoatesino	Brunello, Cabernet
Borro Cepparello	Isole e Olena	Sangiovese
Bruno di Rocca	Montefili	Cabernet, Sangioveto
Cabreo	Ruffino	Cabernet, Sangiovese
Ca' del Pazzo	Caparzo	Cabernet, Brunello
Cetinaia	San Polo in Rosso	Sangiovese
Codirosso	Fattoria di Vistarenni	Sangiovese
Coltassala	Castello di Volpaia	Sangioveto, Mammolo
Concerto	Castello di Fonterutoli	Sangiovese, Cabernet
Flaccianello	Fontodi	Sangiovese
Fontalloro	Fattoria di Felsina	Sangiovese
Ghiaie della Furba	Contini-Bonacossi	Cabernet Sauvignon, Franc and Merlot
Grifi	Avignonese	Prugnolo, Cabernet
I Sodi di San Niccolò	Castellare	Sangioveto, Canaiolo, Malvasia
Niccolo' di Uzzano	Castello di Uzzano	Sangiovese
Le Corte	Castello di Querceto	Sangiovese
La Pergole Torte	Montevertine	Sangiovese
Palazzo Altesi	Altesino	Brunello
Sammarco	Castello di Rampolla	Cabernet, Sangiovese
Sangioveto	Badia a Coltibuono	Sangioveto
Sassicaia	Marchesi Incisa della Rocchetta	Cabernet Sauvignon, Cabernet Franc
Solaia	Marchesi Antinori	Cabernet, Sangiovese

Solatio Basilica	Villa Cafaggio	Sangiovese
Tavernelle	Villa Banfi	Cabernet Sauvignon
Tignanello	Marchesi Antinori	Sangiovese, Cabernet
Vinattieri Rosso	Vinattieri	Sangioveto, Brunello

PREDICATO DI BITURICA

This is a new DOC appellation established to secure a place under the umbrella of Italian wine laws for Tuscan blends based on Cabernet. The somewhat unfortunate latinate term means "enhanced by Cabernet". The minimum requirement calls for 30% Cabernet. Some of these new wines contain as much as 85% Cabernet.

WHITE WINES

In Tuscany white wines have always occupied a distant second place to the reds. But in recent years white wine vinification has made great progress. However, a complaint is that the new-style Tuscan white wine has become too neutral, without much perfume or flavor. So now we are seeing the pendulum swing back toward more aromatic whites of distinct personality. Most of these richer whites are based on Chardonnay. The ubiquitous Trebbiano grape responsible for so many indifferent white wines is being abandoned by many serious producers.

VERNACCIA DI SAN GIMIGNANO

A dry white DOC wine produced in the hills of San Gimignano from Vernaccia grapes. This golden wine of good ageing capacity traditionally has a strong, distinctive flavor which can take some getting used to. However, as a result of the industry's trend towards pale, clean white wines, some versions of Vernaccia have been stripped of the characteristic bitter almond flavor. Traditionalists like Teruzzi e Puthod reacted to this development by ageing Vernaccia in fresh oak barrels, a practice which is revealing a whole new personality of Vernaccia.

Guicciardini Strozzi
Falchini

Fattoria Il Paradiso
Fattoria di Pietrafitta
Il Palagio
Montenidoli
Pietraserena
Teruzzi e Puthod
La Torre
La Quercia di Racciano

GALESTRO

This is a newly created dry white wine for summer drinking made of Trebbiano and other grapes grown in central Tuscany. It takes its name from the grey rock that is churned up when ground is plowed for the planting of new vines. Although Galestro has been a success in our "lighter-is-better" age, its inventor, Giacomo Tacchis of Antinori, has said that it is not really a wine at all, but simply a winelike beverage. That noted, it must be allowed that Galestro *va giu' molto bene* (goes down nicely) on a hot Tuscan afternoon.

BIANCO DI PITIGLIANO

This is a light, dry wine produced in southern Tuscany to be drunk as young as possible. It is made from a variety of grapes including Greco, Verdicchio, Trebbiano, and Malvasia.

VINI DA TAVOLA

A short survey of new white wines in Tuscany shows the sudden ascendancy of Chardonnay and total absence of Trebbiano, despite its overwhelming presence in Tuscan vineyards.

WINE	**PRODUCERS**	**GRAPES**
Collina di Ama	Castello di Ama	Chardonnay
Cabreo	Ruffino	Chardonnay
Fontanelle	Villa Banfi	Chardonnay

Il Benefizio	Marchesi de' Frescobaldi	Pinot Bianco, Chardonnay
Terre di Tufo	Teruzzi e Puthod	Vernaccia
Marzocco	Avignonesi	Chardonnay
Mariggio	Fontodi	Chardonnay
Le Grance	Tenuta Carpazo	Chardonnay
Cervaro	Villa Antinori	Chardonnay, Grechetto

ROSÉ WINES

Rosé in Tuscany is usually made from Sangiovese, either alone or blended with other varieties. Some are excellent, and it remains a mystery why you don't see more of these perfect summer companions on Tuscan tables.

Artimino
Capezzana
Badia a Coltibuono
Castello San Polo in Rosso
Marchesi de' Frescobaldi
Ruffino
Villa Antinori

VIN SANTO

An amber dessert wine often compared to Sherry but really quite different. This 'holy wine' is made from semi-dried grapes, pressed and sealed in small barrels. The barrels are kept in lofts or attics, where they react to the extremes of summer and winter temperatures, for at least three years. Most of the vin santo found in Tuscany - there is hardly a farmhouse which doesn't produce its own - leaves much to be desired. At its best, however, (like the creamy Avignonesi version with its long cognac-like finish), vin santo is a great wine to be savored. Although usually sweet, vin santo is also being produced as a semi-sweet, almost dry wine. A fascinating dry version - rustic, flavorful, and refined all at once - is made by Frescobaldi. Most vin santo is made from Malvasia, Trebbiano, and Grechetto grapes.

Artimino
Avignonesi
Badia a Coltibuono

Brolio (Ricasoli)
Contini-Bonacossi
Giovanni Cappelli
Aldo Casagni
Castel in Villa
Castellare di Castellina
Castello di Uzzano
Castello di Volpaia
Riccardo Falchini
Fattoria di Barbi
Guicciardini Strozzi
Isole e Olena
Marchesi Antinori
Marchesi de' Frescobaldi
Monte Vertine
Pogliarese
Poggio al Sole
San Giorgio a Lapi
Tenuta Il Poggione
Tenuta La Lellera

SPUMANTE

Tuscan producers have only recently tried their hands at dry sparkling Spumante (with the exception of Antinori which has long been producing the bubbly using northern grapes). Pinot and Chardonnay are favored by some, while others use local varieties such as Vernaccia.

Antinori Brut Nature
Brut di Capezzana
Caparzo Brut Rose'
Cusona Brut (Guicciardini Strozzi)
Falchini Brut
Frescobaldi Brut
Ricasoli Brut

A SELECTION OF TUSCAN WINE PRODUCERS

CASTELLO DI SAN POLO IN ROSSO

The drawing of the castle reproduced here first appeared on a military map of the area in the 1600's. The castle is now a national monument, and the drawing is used as an emblem by the wine estate of Castello San Polo in Rosso.

This is a beautiful property located south of Gaiole in the Chianti Classico zone. San Polo is one of the wineries in Chianti which has been revitalized in the last twenty years through injections of capital and the determination to produce only the finest wines possible. The present owner is Cesare Canessa, a Neapolitan whose family is in the business of antiques and old master paintings. He and his German-born wife Katrin took over the property in 1970. The winemaking at San Polo is directed by Maurizio Castelli, one of the innovative eonologists responsible for the high level of expertise present in Tuscany today. He also guides the viticultural affairs for other top wineries in Tuscany.

The vineyards of San Polo are blessed in summertime with hot days and cool nights, a combination that allows the grapes to mature slowly and to develop a full perfume. An important aspect of the winemaking at San Polo is the rigorous selection of grapes during the harvest. Only fully ripened bunches are picked and pressed. Underdeveloped grapes are left to come along in their own good time. This system makes for a long and laborious harvest, but one which is handsomely repaid by the fine wines that result.

San Polo produces a white wine, a Chianti Classico and a Riserva. Rosa dell'Erta is a rosé made from 100% Sangiovese. The 1989 version has a beautiful color and enchanting aroma of berries. San Polo's top wine is Cetinaia, made from 100% Sangiovese and aged in small barrels of French wood. Cetinaia is produced only in good years and has won a reputation as one of the elite red table wines now produced in Tuscany. Cesare Canessa is not one to get terribly excited by the growing movement towards blending Cabernet into the traditional Tuscan wines. "Sangiovese, is the Tuscan variety", he says, "and always has been. For me, the taste of a Tuscan red is the taste of Sangiovese, and I'm happy to leave it that way." He makes a telling point when he asks, "Can you imagine how the French would react if we suggested they blend Sangiovese into their wines"?

MARCHESI DE' FRESCOBALDI

Since medieval times the Frescobaldi's have been among the most dynamic and important of the Florentine families, with merchants, soldiers, poets and musicians to their credit as well as wine makers.

The Frescobaldi's were particularly successful as bankers, financing various Popes from Nicholas III to Clement V. The expenses of Edward I, King of England, were underwritten by the Frescobaldi Bank. (The King's refusal to pay his bills in the 13th century figures as one of the family's more unpleasant memories). Other illustrious members of the family include the poets Dino and Matthew, and the 17th century composer Girolamo Frescobaldi.

Since the 1300's the Frescobaldis have dedicated themselves primarily to agriculture, especially to the cultivation of vines and olive trees. The Frescobaldi family owns eight farms in four different wine growing regions: in the Chianti zones of Rufina and the Colli Fiorentini near Florence, in the zones of Brunello di Montalcino and Pomino. The sheer variety of terrain, microclimates, and vines found on these estates affords the viticulturists at Frescobaldi marvelous possibilities for research and experimentation.

The recent fashion of planting Chardonnay and Cabernet vines in Tuscany has not exactly taken the Frescobaldi farms by storm. These varieties were first brought to the family's farms from France back in 1855 by Marchese Vittorio degli Albizi. The Marchese was a leader in the development of the viticultural techniques of his day. The marriage that united the Frescobaldi to the Albizi family represented a brilliant coup for the Frescobaldi winemakers.

From the Pomino estate comes Pomino Bianco made from Chardonnay, Pinot Bianco, and Pinot Grigio as well as a red wine called simply Pomino Rosso which is a blend of Cabernet, Sangioveto, Pinot Nero and Merlot. Vineyards from the Nipozzano estate in the Rufina zone yield the red Mormoreto, made from Cabernet Sauvignon and Cabernet Franc which comes under the new appellation of Predicato di Biturica.

The Chianti Riserva from Nipozzano, which also has a touch of Cabernet, is aged two years in wood and at least 9 months in the bottle. It is a somewhat idiosyncratic wine sometimes requiring 10 years of aging before it fully reveals itself.

Also from the Nipozzano estate is a Chianti called Montesodi from a single prized vineyard, a kind of cru within a cru. Aged 20 months in small oak barrels, Montesodi is the most expensive Chianti on the market and possibly the best.

The Nipozzano vineyards range between 400 and 700 meters in altitude with superior drainage and excellent exposure to the sun. With these advantages the Nipozzano vineyards have little to fear from wet autumnal weather. The grapes can be safely left on the vines until they've reached the peak of ripeness and sugar content.

The Frescobaldi farms are becoming increasingly serious about their production of top quality olive oils. Apparently the day is not far off when the experience of fine dining will require that we choose not only the wines to accompany our meal but also the specific kinds of olive oil; as a supplement to the wine list, there will be the olive oil list to master.

MONTE VERTINE

Some twenty years Sergio Manetti bought a country house near Radda in Chianti as a refuge from the rigors of directing his iron and steel concern. His first attempts at wine-making at Monte Vertine turned out so well that he sold his industrial interests and devoted his energy to the ancient art of vinification.

Signor Manetti was the first to produce the new-style 100% Sangiovese wine with his Le Pergole Torte in 1977. One of the finest expressions of what Sangiovese is capable of in Tuscany, Le Pergole Torte has inspired other producers to bring out their own versions of 100% Sangiovese wines. (Most notable among these are Cetinaia, Flaccianello, and Sangioveto, made by San Polo, Fontodi and Badia a Coltibuono, respectively). These wines were created as a reaction against the old Chianti formula which called for a significant addition of white grapes.

Signor Manetti explains that in the old days Chianti vineyards were interspersed with grain which enriched the soil and produced potent black grapes. Since the need back then was for a light Chianti to be drunk young, a significant addition of white grapes tempered the austere character of Sangiovese.

Monte Vertine has remained small with only 7.5 hectares of vineyards and has no plans to expand. The philosophy is simple: to produce the best wines possible using the traditional vines of Tuscany. There is not the slightest chance that any foreign vines will be planted here. "Aren't there enough Cabernets and Chardonnays in the world?" asks Sergio Manetti, amazed by the modern tendency toward overkill.

The excellent basic red wine of the estate is called simply Monte Vertine. Along with Sangiovese grapes, it includes some of the traditional red varietal Canaiolo. Il Sodaccio is a more refined version of the same blend as is Il Cannaio, which is produced solely for the Enoteca Pinchiorri restaurant in Florence. A white wine called *M*, made from the Tuscan workhorses Trebbiano and Malvasia, is aged some time in oak.

At age 70, Sergio Manetti seems slightly bemused by his

success as a viniculturist. His satisfaction is apparent when he speaks of his wines as his children. His real children are all involved in the business, as well as son-in-law, Klaus Johann Riemitz. Sergio Manetti delights in his role as defender of the Chianti tradition. For the last 40 years he has been collecting household objects, farming tools and winemaking machines used by Chianti farmers up until the postwar years. They are displayed in a small museum on the property. Lest anyone think that the Leonardos and Michelangelos sprang out of nowhere, here is proof of the very high level of craftmanship and ingenuity exercised by common Tuscans working the land.

The Manettis will be happy to open the museum to small groups, but ask that visits be booked several days in advance and only for weekdays. Tel: 0577/738099

SAN FELICE

The estate of San Felice, which encompasses the beautiful village of the same name, is located in the southeast corner of the Chianti Classico zone. It has a long tradition of vine growing.

The management at San Felice is ideally Janus-faced, looking deeply into the history of Tuscan winemaking at the same time it attempts to plot the future of its wines.

Over 15 years ago the firm's managing director, Enzo Morganti, joined with the Universities of Florence, Siena, and Piacenza to do research on grape varieties and techniques of production. The Cabernet Sauvignon vines planted back then have since matured and contribute to the wine Vigorello, 85% Sangiovese and 15% Cabernet, aged in barrique and bottle, which was the first of the new-style Tuscan table wines to exploit this blend. Vigorello is a lovely wine with good depth and complexity, and lots of fruit.

San Felice is also involved in a project to save and revitalize the forgotten vines of Tuscany which fell out of favor when they weren't included in the Chianti formula set by Baron Ricasoli back in the last century. A selection of these varieties, with delightful names such as "good friend", "wet the bed", "cat's balls" and "prieststrangler", have been planted on the San Felice Estate.

Someday one or more of these Tuscan varieties may play a part in the future of Chianti wines. The DOCG regulations currently allow for the addition of 10% of ANY red grapes the producer chooses to top off the 90% of Sangiovese required. At San Felice the feeling is that a little bit of Cabernet goes a long way because of its strong "tinting" characteristics.

San Felice obviously has nothing against Cabernet Sauvignon. Their Predicato di Biturica contains a minimum of 30%. But these blends show that even a small addition of Cabernet Sauvignon changes the traditional character of Chianti beyond recognition.

San Felice's Chianti Classico Riserva called Poggio Rosso is an expression of an ideal Chianti based on tradition. Poggio Rosso is made entirely of Sangiovese or varietal clones grown on a small *cru* vineyard which is tended with the utmost care.

Meanwhile the resort village of San Felice continues to grow. A first-class restaurant has just opened near the tennis courts. Surrounded by flowers and vineyards this serene spot is proving popular, especially among German visitors.

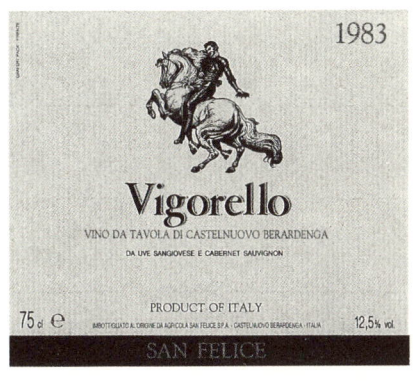

CHIANTI GEOGRAFICO

With the emphasis in Tuscany increasingly on the production of quality wines and with the costs of achieving that quality soaring, what is a small undercapitalized producer to do?

One solution found by 125 vineyard owners in the communes of Castellina, Radda and Gaiole was to sign on with the winemaking cooperative called Geografico. The firm was founded in 1961 by Carlo Sderci and Guido Iappini, two wine-loving Sienese bank directors. (The name Geografico was chosen in recognition of the fact that these three geographical zones formed the first league of Chianti wine growers back in the 13th century).

In the hazardous world of vine cultivation membership in a cooperative such as Geografico can offer the small grower vital security. Of course the individual vineyard owners must surrender their identities as well as the joys of sipping their very own wines. However, in the case of Geografico the member growers can take considerable consolation in the knowledge that the directors of the cooperative are committed to the quality end of the market employing as their chief enologist the well-respected Vittorio Fiore.

An advantage enjoyed by the wine master at Geografico is the opportunity to pick and choose grapes from the various vineyards to suit his needs. What this wealth of choice can mean was demonstrated in 1984, generally a disastrous year for Tuscan wine. Springtime rain and high humidity, followed by really rotten weather in September, reduced a great many vineyards to a condition not conducive to quality winemaking. With few exceptions the only grapes worth vinifying were those from high altitude vineyards with excellent drainage. Most producers had to choose between severely lowered yields or wines of much lower quality. Because of Geografico's enormous grape pool the firm came through the bad year very nicely, bottling some 7000 hectoliters of good Chianti, over half the usual yield.

The great challenge for Geografico is to make certain that the many member vineyards are being looked after according to the standards set by Sig. Fiore. To that end a young enologist constantly makes the rounds inspecting vineyards and counseling owners. Of course if an estate's fruit for some reason doesn't measure up, it can simply be rejected for that year's vinification.

Geografico's wines include Chianti Classico, Chianti Riserva from the estate of Montegiachi, and the new light wines Galestro and Sarmento. After misfiring in 1985 with its first Predicato di Biturica (a new appellation for a blend of Cabernet Sauvignon and Sangiovese), Geografico's 1986 version of 85% Cabernet turned out splendidly, representing yet another success for Cabernet in Tuscany.

Geografico also produces two of the best known appellations in Italy, Vino Nobile di Montepulciano, (Geografico's version being called Cerraia), and the traditional king of Tuscan reds, Brunello di Montalcino.

Two well-known estates have arranged with the cooperative to retain their names under the Geografico label. The Chianti Classico wines of Castello di Fagnano and La Contessa di Radda consist of grapes from specific vineyards on those estates. They are vinified, bottled and marketed by Geografico.

CASTELLO DI UZZANO

The Castle of Uzzano is situated on a hilltop near Greve in the heart of Chianti. Built on foundations that are probably of Etruscan and Roman origin, the castle was enlarged during the medieval period and finally became a villa in the 17th century.

The castle itself has been the site of a fair amount of Florentine history. One of the first lords of the castle, Niccolo' da Uzzano, was an important leader during the Renaissance. In Machiavelli's account of the times, Da Uzzano figures prominently as a successful opponent of the Medici's rise to power. Today the Uzzano estate is owned by Count Briano Castelbarco Albani whose mother's family acquired it in 1641.

The archives of Francesco Datini, the famous merchant of Prato, document that the wines of Uzzano were noted for their excellence as long ago as 1398 when Datini's company was already shipping them abroad.

Today Uzzano's reputation for fine wines is higher than ever. The winemaking, as well as everything else at Uzzano, is looked after by Marion de Jacobert who is a stickler for quality. She has closely studied Tuscan winemaking methods, old and new, and has put back into pratice some of the forgotten ways. For instance, the Uzzano estate has returned to the old method of planting broad beans and sainfoin among the vines. These crops are plowed into the soil as compost, or green manure, to enrich the mineral content and, in turn, the vines themselves. Uzzano employs a second summer pruning to give the grapes more light for fuller maturation and uses only organic manure.

Uzzano produces Chianti Classico and Riserva wines as well as the special vino da tavola Niccolò da Uzzano, a red made solely from Sangioveto grapes and aged in small barrels of three different types of wood. Fresco di Governo is a red wine made from Canaiolo grapes according to the old governo process involving a second and natural fermentation. It is best consumed while still young.

Uzzano white wine has no traces of Trebbiano and Malvasia, the usual Tuscan white grapes which are now fighting an uphill battle for respectablility on the world market. Instead, this is a white made up entirely of "foreigners": Chardonnay, Gewürztraminer, Pinot Bianco, and Sauvignon.

Pharmalogical tests conducted by the University of Florence have turned up a curiosity: the red wines of Uzzano are apparently free of histamines. This finding ought to be of interest to anyone who suffers allergic reactions to the histamines in red wines. The Castello di Uzzano also produces olive oil, honey and grappa, all three of premium quality.

The extensive gardens around the castle have also been revitalized in recent years. The flora includes a baby Sequoia shipped from California in the last century. Travelers might like to know that Uzzano offers wine tastings by appointment, as well as group dinners in the courtyard of the castle. Several luxury flats around the courtyard of the castle are also available by the week. Tel: (055) 854032

TENUTA SAN GUIDO (SASSICAIA)

If Hollywood ever decides to make a film about a wine the star would have to be Sassicaia. At least, it would if the film were set in the 1970's, for that was the decade in which Sassicaia seduced the wine world and became the Tuscan red with a cult following.

The plot is something along the lines of the ugly duckling that turns into a swan, or the forgotten Cinderella who becomes a princess.

The Marchese Incisa della Rocchetta had dreamed of planting Cabernet vines at his coastal estate near Bolgheri (south of Pisa) ever since acquiring a taste for fine Bordeaux as a young man. He was convinced that he could produce a fine Cabernet in Tuscany, perhaps because he had once tasted such a wine made by the Dukes of Salviati on their Tuscan estates. Wine experts informed of the project declared that the Marchese was suffering from delusion since the terrain around Bolgheri had never produced anything but defective wine, and besides, it was common knowledge that decent Cabernet couldn't be made near the sea.

The first attempts were somewhat disastrous; local farmers pronounced the wine dreadful, in fact, undrinkable. The Marchese persisted with his rustic home-brew version of Cabernet for some twenty years, slowly improving the quality but never considering his wine fit for anything but family consumption.

Then, in the 1960's, when a young vineyard protected from salty off-shore winds began to yield fruit, and serious modern winemaking techniques were introduced, a different wine began to emerge and a startling discovery was made. This Cabernet from the coast of Tuscany called Sassicaia (80% Sauvignon, 20% Franc) was a big, obstinate, complex wine which required years of ageing before being transformed into a superb rich nectar capable of conquering the wine world. Slowly Sassicaia was leaked onto the world market, aided by the Antinori family, cousins of the Marchese. In 1975 Sassicaia, once undrinkable and scorned, defied the experts by taking first prize at a prestigious London competition as the world's best Cabernet for that year.

Here is how Nicolas Belfrage, master of wine, describes Sassicaia in his book *Life Beyond Lambrusco*. "Sassicaia starts out life very concentrated and essence-of-blackcurrant, with a hefty structure which holds the fruit together in a tight rich knot until about the tenth year when it begins to open out, becoming velvety, opulent, almost liqueur-like".

Now there's no end to the list of the rich and famous who scheme and plead for just one case of Sassicaia, whose production is limited, never exceeding 100,000 bottles per year.

Sassicaia is destined to be of lasting historical importance to the Tuscan wine busines for it was the forerunner of several vital trends: it was the first Cabernet to emerge in Tuscany, the first fine Tuscan wine aged in small wooden barriques, and the first so-called table wine to command both world attention and a high price.

RECIPES FROM FLORENTINE RESTAURANTS

PASTA E CECI
Pasta and chick pea soup

OSTERIA N.1

For five:

- 500 gr. chick peas, already cooked (boiled)
- 50 gr. tomato cubes or pulp
- 1 onion
- 1 carrot
- 1 celery stalk
- 4 cloves garlic
- 2 small branches of fresh rosemary, if available (otherwise use 1 table spoon of dried rosemary)
- 1/2 broth cube
- olive oil as needed
- salt and peper
- 200-300 gr pasta (smaller forms are better for soup)

Chop the carrot, celery and onion into very fine pieces. Pour enough olive oil into a saucepan to cover the bottom and gently sauté the vegetables until they begin to turn color. Add then the tomato pulp, followed by the chick peas (they should already be rather soft), the broth cube and 1 cup of water, salt and pepper.

Let the mixture simmer for at least half an hour, then pass it through a food mill and return to heat.

In another small saucepan sauté the garlic cloves with the rosemary in some olive oil. Stir this olive oil (removing the garlic and rosemary) into the chick pea blend. Add the pasta and boil it in the chick pea purée as you would in water (do not drain when done). Serve this soup either hot or cold, as preferred.

FARFALLINE ALLE NOCI
Butterfly pasta with walnut and sausage sauce

Osteria N.1

For six:

- 600 gr. butterfly shaped pasta
- 300 gr. walnuts
- 100 gr. grated parmesan cheese
- 2 Italian sausage (sweet)
- 1 cup whipping cream
- 1 pat of butter
- 1 tablespoon olive oil
- 1 tablespoon olive oil salt, pepper and grated nutmeg to taste

Mince the walnuts and the sausage. Sauté them in a saucepan in the oil for 3-4 minutes. Add the butter, cheese, cream, salt, pepper and nutmeg and let the sauce boil until it reduces a bit. Stir the already cooked pasta into the sauce and top with some grated parmesan cheese before serving.

CRESPELLE ALLA FIORENTINA
Crepes filled with spinach and ricotta

Ristorante "13 Gobbi"

Batter for crepes:
- 60 gr. flour
- 2 eggs
- 1 cup milk
- pinch of salt
- 1 pat of butter, melted

Filling:
- 40 gr. spinach (cooked and chopped fine)
- 200 gr. ricotta cheese
- 2 tablespoons grated parmesan cheese
- 1 egg
- grated nutmeg
- salt and pepper

Béchamel sauce topping:
- 50 gr. flour
- 50 gr. butter
- 1/2 liter milk
- 3 tablespoons smooth tomato sauce

Prepare the batter for the crepes. Blend the eggs with the flour and the salt, then add the milk and the butter little by little. Let the batter rest for 45 minutes.

Mix together the spinach with the other filling ingredients. In a frying pan (or crêpe pan) prepare 8-10 small crêpes. Lay them flat and form a roll of filling in the middle, then wrap the crepe to form a cannelloni type roll (it should not be too full).

Prepare the béchamel by melting the butter in a heavy bottomed pan. Add the cold milk in a steady stream, stirring continually until the mixture is rather thick (be patient).

Pour this sauce over the crespelle in a casserole or other pan that may go into the oven. Dot the béchamel with the tomato sauce and heat in a hot oven for 15-20 minutes. Serve hot.

RISOTTO VERDE
Green risotto

OSTERIA GANINO

Boil rice in salted water for 12 minutes (Uncle Ben's Long Grain rice recommended). Boil fresh spinach in water with a pinch of baking soda to retain green color. Purée the spinach in a blender or food mill.

In a bowl stir the spinach with a pinch of salt, a bit of butter, enough cream to make a thick sauce and parmesan cheese.

Add the cooked rice and blend well. Serve with parmesan cheese.

PASSATO DI PEPERONI GIALLI
Purée of Yellow Peppers

CIBREO

For six:
- 4 yellow bell peppers
- 6 potatoes
- 2 bay leaves
- 1 cup milk
- 1/2 cup olive oil
- salt
- meat broth (300/400 gr. boiling meat, 1 piece of tail, 1 broth bone, 1 onion, 1 celery stalk, 1 carrot)
- 1 onion, 1 celery stalk, 1 carrot

Wash the yellow peppers and cut into small pieces. Dice the potatoes. Chop the onion, celery and carrot into small pieces and sautee in the olive oil until very slightly colored. Add to the same pan the potatoes and peppers and enough broth to cover.
Stir, add some salt and boil until the potatoes are cooked. Pass the mixture through a food mill or blender, removing pepper skins if necessary. Reheat the purée until it returns to a boil, remove from heat and add the bay leaves and milk.
Serve hot with crusty bread and grated cheese.

SFORMATO DI CARCIOFI
Crustless, Artichoke Quiche

TRATTORIA LA BARAONDA

For six:

- 10 large artichokes
- 50 gr. butter
- 50 gr. flour (2 heaping spoonfuls)
- 5 eggs
- 1/2 liter milk
- grated parmesan cheese
- salt
- 2 cloves garlic, whole

Clean the artichokes (remove all tough outer leaves, pare stem and cut in half). Cook immediately in a closed pot with 3 tablespoons of olive oil and 2 cloves of garlic until very tender. Remove garlic.

In the meantime, prepare a béchamel sauce. Melt butter in a saucepan (taking care not to let it burn), and add the flour, stirring continually. Then, still stirring, add the milk, little by little, until the mixture attains a thick consistency. Let cool.

Pass the artichokes through a food mill and stir this pulp with 5 egg yolks, the béchamel sauce, 2 spoonfuls of cheese and salt. Mix well.

Beat the egg whites until they form peaks. Fold them delicately into artichoke mixture with a wooden spoon.

Pour batter into a buttered angel food cake tin and bake for approximately 40 minutes at 180°.

FILETTO AL PEPE VERDE
Green peppercorn fillet

TRATTORIA PENNELLO

Flour and salt a steak fillet. Fry very lightly in butter.

Remove from pan, let butter drip off and then pour brandy over the steak. In the pan, make a sauce with 2 teaspoons of mustard, 1/2 cup of cream, l teaspoon of green peppercorns and 2 teaspoons Worcestershire sauce. When this is hot and creamy, return the steak to the pan and finish cooking it in the sauce.

The fillet should be rather thick and served medium rare.

BISTECCA ALLA FIORENTINA
Florentine steak

BUCA LAPI

This beefsteak is a classic Florentine specialty.

The cut is a T-bone and usually weighs from 600-800 grams. The chef at Buca Lapi grills the 2 cm. high steaks over organic charcoal on both sides until the outside is crusty (never puncturing the meat with a fork). Tradition dictates that the steak be salted only after grilling and that it become crusty outside and remain rare inside ("al sangue").

BRACIOLINE DI MANZO ALLA CHIANTIGIANA
Chianti Beef Steaks

RISTORANTE "13 GOBBI"

- 1 tablespoon chopped carrots
- 1 tablespoon chopped onion
- 1/2 tablespoon chopped Italian parsley
- 1 cup peeled tomatoes
- 1 ean beef steaks, thinly sliced
- 2 cups red wine

In a saucepan, lightly sauté the chopped carrot, onion and parsley in olive oil. Add tomato and bring to a simmer. Add a cup of red wine.
Fry the steaks over a high flame in olive oil and add the other cup of red wine at the end of cooking time. Add the meat then to the pan of tomato sauce and continue cooking for 15 minutes.
Very good served with fagioli all'uccelletto.

BRACIOLE DI MANZO DELLA CASA
House Steak

COCO LEZZONE

- steak for frying
- 1 cup breadcrumbs
- olive oil (for frying)
- 1 cup tomato sauce
- 1 clove garlic
- sage
- rosemary
- salt and pepper

Dip the steaks in beaten egg and then in the breadcrumbs. Fry in olive oil.

Remove the steaks from the pan and flavor the same oil with the garlic clove. Remove garlic, return the steaks to the pan, cover with tomato sauce, sage and rosemary and bring it to a boil. Reduce slightly. Salt and pepper and serve hot.

SCALOPPINE SAN MINIATO
Veal cutlet with truffles

QUATTRO STAGIONI

For six:

- 600 gr. veal
- 150 gr. Fontina cheese
- 50 gr. white truffles
- 50 gr. butter
- 100 gr. cooking cream
- salt, pepper
- 1/2 cup cognac

Slice the veal into 50 gr. cutlets and pound lightly. Flour and fry in butter until well-colored. Pour cognac over them and let evaporate. Add cream and bring to simmer. Put the veal and cream in a pyrex dish (suitable for oven use) and cover them with the cheese slices. Put in hot oven for 5 minutes. Remove and cover with the truffles, cut in slices. Serve immediately.

COLLO DI POLLO RIPIENO
Stuffed chicken neck

Cibreo

For six:

- 6 de-boned chicken necks
- 500 gr. beef, ground twice
- 1 egg
- soft, white part of homemade bread (not crust)
- 1 cup milk
- 100 gr. grated parmesan
- grated lemon rind to taste

For mayonnaise:
- 3 egg yolks
- 8 oz. olive oil "extra vergine"
- juice of 1-2 lemons

Soak the bread white in the milk. Put the ground beef, the parmesan cheese, egg, salt and lemon rind in a bowl. When the bread is completely soaked in the milk, add it to the other ingredients without squeezing it too much. Mix well with your hands until well blended.
At this point, fill the chicken necks with the mixture as if you were filling small sacks, talking care to push the mixture to the bottom without leaving pockets of air.
Close the open end with toothpicks or kitchen string. Boil the necks for 15 minutes, if possible, in meat broth. When cooked, cut each neck into slices (1 neck per person).
Blend the egg yolks slowly with a wooden spoon in a bowl. After a minute or so, begin to add the oil, drop by drop. Continue stirring. As the mayonnaise begin to thicken, continue to add the oil in a steady, thin stream. When mayonnaise has achieved its characteristic creamy consistency, stir in lemon juice to taste.
Serve meat slices at room temperature with mayonnaise.

HARRY'S SHRIMPS
(not Tuscan, but good all the same)

HARRY'S BAR

For six:

Take shrimps out of their shells. Cook briefly in a pan with butter, salt and pepper. Burn them with good French Cognac.

Sauce:
- 2 tablespoons of butter
- 1 tablespoon of flour
- 1/2 cup of fish broth
- 1/2 cup dry white wine
- 1/2 cup of heavy milk cream
- 3 egg yolks well beaten
- 1 scallion onion chopped
- pinch of salt
- pinch of pepper
- juice of half a lemon

Melt butter, mix in flour, add fish broth, then wine, then add the cream, stirring slowly all the time. Add the egg yolks slowly to the lemon juice, salt, pepper and cook until thickened.

Pour this sauce on the shrimps, add some grated parmesan cheese and keep them in the oven 7 minutes then serve with rice.

Prepare in a large pan: 1 tablespoon of butter with 1/4 onion chopped fine and cook for 2 minutes. Add 3 cups of rice, 3 good cups of consommé , salt, and let the rice cook in a well covered pot for 18 minutes. Let the rice stand for 20 minutes to dry and sprinkle with a little curry powder and serve.

TRANCIA DI SALMONE ALLA GRENOBLESE
Salmon steak alla Grenoblese

Il Profeta

Lightly dust a salmon steak in some flour and sauté in a tablespoon of olive oil. Add 2 or 3 whole capers and the pulp of 1/2 a lemon, chopped into small pieces. Add enough broth, bit by bit, to create a sauce to pour over the fish. Serve hot.

SCAMPI ALL'UCCELLETTO
Prawn in tomato and sage sauce

Trattoria Cammillo

For four:

- 400 gr. prawn tails, shelled and cleaned
- 300 gr. cannelloni beans, boiled
- 400-500 gr. peeled tomato
- chopped garlic
- chopped sage
- olive oil

Lightly brown the prawns in oil, garlic and sage. Add the tomatoes and beans and bring to simmer. Let reduce and serve hot.

GAMBERONI ALLO SPIEDO
Skewered Prawns

ENOTECA PINCHIORRI

For four:

- 12 large prawns
- 12 thin slices of smoked bacon
- 8 whole bay leaves
- 2 tableespoons olive oil
- 4 endives
- butter
- salt and pepper
- 4 long wooden skewers

Clean the prawns, removing the heads. Wash and dry. Roll each one with a slice of bacon. Put the prawns on a skewer alternating with a bay leaf.
Continue this process until each stick has 3 prawns and 2 bay leaves on it.
Sauté the skewers in a pan with oil until the prawns are cooked.
Julienne the endive and sauté in a pan with butter. Add salt and pepper to taste.
To present this dish, place the endive on a hot plate.
Remove the skewer and place the prawns on top of the endive.
Garnish and sprinkle with olive oil.

TRIGLIE ALLA VIAREGGINA
Red Mullet with Porcini Mushrooms

ENOTECA PINCHIORRI

For four:

- 600 gr. red mullet, cleaned and deboned
- 35-40 gr. dried porcini mushrooms
- 1-2 cloves garlic
- 1-2 pieces shallots
- 5 gr. capers
- 5 gr. anchovy paste
- salt and pepper
- olive oil
- 100 ml chicken stock

Soak the porcini mushrooms in water for at least 6 hours. Then, remove the mushrooms, strain the water and put it aside.

Chop the mushrooms, garlic, shallots and capers very fine. In some oil, sauté these ingredients. Add the anchovy paste.

Then add the chicken stock and a little of the water from the porcini. Let cook for 5-10 minutes.

Remove and blend together. The consistency of this sauce should be rather thick, almost a purée.

Season the red mullet and either pan fry them or steam them.

Place the sauce on a hot plate and top with the fish. Sprinkle with olive oil. Garnish and serve.

SPUMONE AL CIOCCOLATO
Chocolate "Ice Cream"

Trattoria La Baraonda

- 60 gr. butter
- 5 eggs
- 200 gr. very dark chocolate in squares
- 2 Tb. powdered sugar

Melt the chocolate in a double boiler. When it becomes a smooth cream, add the butter cut into small pieces, and melt completely. Remove from heat and add the egg yolks. Mix well with a wooden spoon.

Beat the egg whites with the powdered sugar until peaks form. Add these to the chocolate liquid. This step must be done very carefully, but quickly, because the egg whites may fall. The Baraonda chef recommends using a wooden spoon with an upward and downward motion. Refrigerate for 4 hours before serving.

OTHER TUSCAN RECIPES

CROSTINI
Paté on toast

- 4 chicken livers
- 4 anchovy fillets
- 50 gr. butter
- 1 teaspoon capers
- 1/4 cup Marsala or Madeira
- salt
- bread (Italian style or other homemade type)

Brown the cleaned livers in 25 gr. of butter. Afterwards, pour the Marsala on the livers and cook until it evaporates. Remove from heat and discard bay leaf.
Put chicken livers, anchovies and capers on cutting board and chop very finely (but do not mince the ingredients). Put the mixture back in the pan and cook for several more minutes. Add salt.
Cut bread into small slices (6-7 mm high).
Toast them lightly in the oven and allow to cool. Spread a little butter on each slice and top with pate.

(For a different taste, the Marsala may be replaced with a very small amount of chicken broth, to be added when the mixture is returned to the cooking pan).

PANZANELLA
Summer bread salad

- 2-3 very ripe tomatoes
- 1 large red onion
- 1 cucumber
- 8-10 large fresh basil leaves, torn
- olive oil and vinegar to dress the salad
- salt and pepper
- 1/2 Kg. Tuscan bread or other homemade hard type, several days old.

Soak the bread in very cold water for 20 minutes, then squeeze the bread to remove excess liquid and crumble

into a bowl.
Cut the onion, tomatoes and cucumber and place on the bread.
Tear the basil leaves and put them on top of the vegetables. Cover the bowl and place in refrigerator for at least 2 hours. When ready to serve, season with salt, pepper, oil and vinegar, mix thoroughly and serve.

FAGIOLI ALL'UCCELLETTO
White beans in tomato sauce

- 1 kg fresh cannellini beans (or substitute), already cooked
- 1 kg fresh or peeled tomatoes (without skins or seeds)
- 1 small handful sage leaves, chopped
- 2 cloves garlic, chopped
- olive oil
- salt and pepper

In a saucepan (preferably of terra cotta) saute lightly the garlic and the sage leaves in oil. Pour in the crushed tomatoes and let simmer for 5 minutes. Add the beans and simmer for another 15 minutes. Add salt and pepper and serve hot. These beans are cooked in a way similar to that used in cooking small birds, 'all'uccelletto.' They are frequently served with Italian sausages.

SPAGHETTI ALLA CARRETTIERA
Spaghetti in a hot tomato sauce

- 1-2 cloves garlic
- 1 handful of Italian parsley leaves
- 1-2 small hot red dried peppers chopped (if already crumbled, use a pinch, or to taste)
- 1 large can of peeled tomatoes
- olive oil
- salt and pepper

Chop the parsley and garlic very fine (the Italians use a two-handled crescent-shaped cutter called a 'mezzaluna' which is very handy for this sort of job). Sauté the garlic and parsley in a couple of tablespoons of olive oil and add the hot peppers.

Take care not to let the garlic brown. Add the tomatoes and their juice and bring to a simmer. Turn down heat, salt and pepper the sauce and let it simmer for 15 minutes, or until at least partially reduced (it should be rather thick).

Toss with previously cooked spaghetti and serve.

PENNE ALLA FIESOLANA
Penne with cream and ham sauce

- 350 gr. penne
- 50 gr. Prosciutto ham, cut into small squares
- 10 gr. (1 tablespoon) flour
- 10 gr. butter
- 1/4 liter milk
- 100 gr. cooking cream
- 1 tablespoon grated parmesan
- handful Italian parsley leaves
- olive oil
- salt and pepper

Prepare a very liquid béchamel sauce with the flour, butter, milk, salt and pepper (see recipe for Crespelle alla Fiorentina for instructions). Add the cream and parmesan cheese.

Brown the prosciutto very lightly in a tablespoon of olive oil. Add the béchamel and stir well.

Add the already cooked penne pasta to this pan and toss with the sauce. Sprinkle with chopped parsley (optional) and serve.

RISOTTO DI MARE
Seafood risotto

- 300 gr. rice Arborio
- 300 gr. mussels
- 300 gr. clams
- 300 gr. shrimp
- 200 gr. small cuttlefish
- 3 tablespoons olive oil
- 2 cloves garlic
- salt, pepper
- parsley
- basil

Clean mussles and clams. Put in a pot over high heat until they open. Shell and clean shrimps. With shells, prepare a broth in 3/4 liter water. Clean cuttlefish. Remove mussels and clams from shells (leave a few for decoration). In a pot heat oil, basil, crush the garlic with salt and sauté for several minutes over low heat. Add parsley, sauté briefly. Add rice, stir to combine with the other flavors. Add seafood, salt and pepper. Stir continually so that it won't stick. Add every so often some strained shrimp broth. The rice is done when tender. Serve hot, garnished with parsley.

"PAPPARDELLE"
Pasta with rabbit/hare sauce

- 1 rabbit (or hare), cleaned and quartered
- 1 stalk of celery
- 1 carrot
- 1 onion
- 1 tablespoon flour
- sage
- 1/2 cup chopped tomato
- salt and pepper
- 1/2 cup red wine
- 1/4 cup broth

Put the rabbit pieces in a pan with a small amount of olive oil and butter. Cook over a very small flame in a closed pot

until the rabbit's juices begin to flow.
Salt and pepper the rabbit.
Meanwhile, chop fine the celery, carrot, onion, sage.
Sauté them in a seperate pan in olive oil for several minutes.
Add them to the rabbit and sprinkle all the ingredients lightly with the flour. Continue to cook very slowly.
Add the wine and let it simmer off. Then add the broth and the tomatoes. Cook for an hour or so over a very low flame. When the rabbit is very tender, cut the meat off the bones and stir it into the sauce.
Serve over "pappardelle" homemade egg pasta strips, similar to tagliatelle.

PETTO DI POLLO ALLA FIORENTINA
Chicken Breast Florentine

- 2 chicken breasts, cut in half
- flour for coating
- butter for frying
- salt and pepper

Salt and pepper the chicken breasts and toss them in flour. Melt the butter in a frying pan and add the chicken when hot. Fry the breasts quickly on each side until brown. Then cover the pan and reduce the heat. Leave the chicken to cook for another 20 minutes.
Serve hot. If desired, the juices may be poured over the chicken before serving.

PEPERONATA
Mixed bell peppers in tomato sauce

- 1 onion
- 1 garlic clove
- 1 green bell pepper
- 1 red bell pepper
- 1 yellow (or orange) bell pepper
- salt and pepper
- 800 gr. peeled tomatoes

Chop the onion and garlic clove very fine. Remove the inner seed core from the peppers and slice them lengthwise into thin strips. Sauté the onion and garlic in olive oil until golden and add the pepper slices. Toss in oil.
Add the tomatoes and a glass of white wine.
Salt and pepper and let cook a half hour, adding if necessary several spoonfuls of water or hot broth.
Serve hot or cold.

PATATE ARROSTO
Roasted potatoes with Rosemary

- 8 large firm potatoes
- 2 tablespoons chopped fresh rosemary (use less if dried)
- 3 tablespoons olive oil
- 2 garlic cloves, cut in half
- salt and pepper

Peel and cut the potatoes into similar sized pieces and in a roasting pan mix the rosemary, garlic and olive oil together. Add the potatoes and stir so that they are completely covered with the oil.
Roast in the oven at 400°F/190°C, turning them frequently so they brown evenly. Remove the garlic cloves when they become soft. Cook until well browned. Salt (and pepper) as they come out of oven.
Serve hot, with meat or as you would roast potatoes.

BISCOTTI DI PRATO
(Hard almond cookies from Prato)

- 500 g flour
- 500 g sugar
- 4 eggs
- 1 teaspoon baking soda
- 1/2 teaspoon salt
- 250 g shelled almonds
- teaspoon vanilla
- 1 egg yolk

Mix the eggs and sugar together. When well blended, add all the other ingredients. Form two or three long loaves and let them rest for an hour. Brush each with some egg yolk. Bake the loaves at 180' until relatively hard (but not too hard). Cut each loaf into diagonal slices of about 3/4 inch each. Turn these biscuits onto one side and return to the oven for a few more minutes.

TIRAMISU
("Pick-me-up")

- 3 eggs, separated
- 1 cup sugar
- 1/2 lb. mascarpone cheese
- Lady finger cookies
- 6 oz. semisweet chocolate bits (optional)
- coffee, cold
- rum/brandy

Blend yolks with sugar until the granules are somewhat absorbed. Add the mascarpone and stir well. Stir in the chocolate bits.

Whip the egg whites until they form peaks. Fold them into the cheese mixture.

Put the coffee and rum into a small bowl dip the cookies, one by one into this liquid. Arrange them so that they cover the bottom of a high-edged serving dish. Spoon enough of the mascarpone mixture onto the cookies to cover. Place another layer of soaked cookies on top and continue alternating cheese and cookie layers until you've filled the dish. Refrigerate for at least two hours. Before serving you may slice some chocolate slivers onto the top.

GLOSSARY

TYPES OF PASTA

tagliatelle	- thin, flat egg pasta ribbons
taglierini	- thin egg pasta ribbons
fettuccine	- long thin pasta noodles
farfalle	- butterfly shaped pasta
ravioli	- spinach and ricotta cheese filled pouches
rigatoni	- large macaroni
tortelli	- "ravioli" with potato filling
tortellini	- small meat-filled pasta pouches
penne	- narrow, diagonally cut macaroni
maccheroni	- macaroni
cannelloni	- large hollow pasta tubes to be stuffed
fusilli	- pasta twists
acciughe	- anchovies
aceto	- vinegar
acqua minerale	- bottled water: gassata is sparkling and naturale is still
acqua non potabile	- undrinkable water
affettati	- sliced meats (prociutto, salami, bologna etc.)
aglio	- garlic
agnello	- lamb
agrumi	- citrus fruit
albicocca	- apricot
alici	- anchovies
alloro	- bay leaf
amaro	- bitter
analcolico	- non-alcoholic
ananas	- pineapple
anatra	- duck
anguilla	- eel
antipasto	- appetizer
antipasto misto	- assorted appetizers
aperitivo	- aperitif
aragosta	- lobster
arancia	- orange
aranciata	- orange soda
aringa	- herring
asparagi	- asparagus
assaggio	- a taste (assaggi - a series of mini portions of primi desserts)

baccalà	- dried salt cod
bacelli	- fava beans (in Tuscany served with pecorino cheese)
basilico	- basil
bavarese	- Bavarian cream
besciamella	- bechamel white sauce
bicchiere	- glass
birra	- beer (birra alla spina - beer on tap)
biscotti	- cookies
bistecca	- beef steak
bresaola	- cured dried beef (or pork)
brioche	- croissant
brodo	- broth
burro	- butter
cacciagione	- game
caffè	- Italian espresso coffee:
caffè ristretto	- very strong espresso
caffè lungo	- espresso with extra water
Hag	- decaffeinated coffee
caffè corretto	- coffee "corrected" with a shot of liquor
caffelatte	- glass of hot milk with a shot of espresso coffee
caffè macchiato	- espresso "stained" with either hot or cold milk
cappuccino	- espresso with steamed, foamy milk
camomilla	- camomile tea
cannellini	- white beans
cantuccini	- hard crescent shaped cookies served often with vin santo
caponata	- eggplant salad
capperi	- capers
carpaccio	- sliced raw beef
castagne	- chestnuts
cavolo	- cabbage
ceci	- chick peas
cena	- dinner
chiuso	- closed (chiuso per ferie - closed for vacation)
ciliegia	- cherry
cinghiale	- wild boar
cioccolato	- chocolate (cioccolata calda - hot chocolate)
cipolla	- onion
cipollina	- pickling onion
cocomero	- watermelon
coda di rospo	- monkfish
colazione	- breakfast

coltello	- knife
coniglio	- rabbit
conto	- bill
contorno	- side dish (usually salad, vegetables or potatoes)
coperto	- cover charge added to bills in majority of restaurants
cozze	- mussels
crostata	- open fruit tart
crostini	- bread slices with chicken liver pate
crudo	- raw (prosciutto crudo - prosciutto: prosciutto cotto - ham)
cucina	- kitchen; cookery
cuore	- heart
dentice	- dentex (Mediterranean fish)
distilleria	- distillery
DOC	- denomination of controlled origin; found on wine labels and applies to wines produced from specified grape varieties cultivated in delimited zones, and according to ageing requirements
DOCG	- guarantees the authenticity and quality of a select group of wines
dolce	- sweet
erbe	- herbs
estera	- imported
fagiano	- pheasant
fagioli	- beans
farina	- flour
farro	- emmer
fave	- fava beans
fegato	- liver
fettunta	- Tuscan garlic bread made with fresh olive oil
fichi	- figs
fichi d'India	- prickly pears
filetto	- fillet
finocchio	- fennel
focaccia	- a flat bread
fontina	- a delicate semi-soft cheese
forchetta	- fork
formaggio	- cheese
fragole	- strawberries
freddo	- cold
frittata	- unfolded omelet
fritto	- fried

fritto misto	- an assortment of fried foods: meat, fish, vegetables, etc.
frutta	- fruit
funghi	- mushrooms
gamberetti	- shrimp
gelato	- Italian ice cream
ghiaccio	- ice
gianduia	- chocolate and hazelnut
gnocchi	- potato dumplings served as first course
gorgonzola	- creamy blue-veined cheese
granchio	- crab
grappa	- spirit distilled from grapeskins remaining from winemaking process
grissini	- breadsticks
Hag	- see "caffè"
insalata	- salad
integrale	- whole wheat (pane integrale - whole wheat bread)
lampone	- raspberries
latte	- milk
lattuga	- lettuce
lenticchie	- lentils
lepre	- hare
lesso	- boiled
limone	- lemon
macedonia	- dessert of sweetened fresh fruits
maiale	- pork
mais	- corn
mandorle	- almonds
manzo	- beef
marroni	- chestnuts
marzolino	- fresh pecorino cheese used in several desserts
mela	- apple
melanzane	- eggplants
melone	- melon; cantaloupe
menta	- mint
merluzzo	- cod
miele	- honey
minestrone	- vegetable soup
mortadella	- pork sausage with cubes of fat
mozzarella	- fresh soft cheese made from buffalo milk (di bufala) or cow milk (fior di latte)
nipitella	- mint-like wild herb
noce	- walnut

nocciola	- hazelnut
olio di oliva	- olive oil
orzo	- barley
ostriche	- oysters
pancetta	- similar to bacon
panino	- sandwich
panna	- cream
panna cotta	- rich cream dessert
parmigiano	- parmesan cheese
pasta	- pasta; pastry; dough
pecorino	- cheese made wholly or partially from sheep's milk, available fresh "fresco" or aged "stagionato"
pepe	- pepper
peperoncini	- hot chili pepper
peperone	- bell pepper
pesce	- fish
pesche	- peaches
pesto	- pasta sauce made with crushed basil, pine nuts pecorino cheese and olive oil
piatto	- plate
piccione	- pigeon
pinoli	- pine nuts
pinzimonio	- raw vegetables dipped in olive oil (celery, artichoke, radish, fennel, etc.)
polenta	- ground cornmeal cooked in boiling water served fresh or later sliced fried and topped with a sauce
polipo	- octopus
pollo	- chicken
polpettone	- meat loaf
polpo	- octopus
pomodoro	- tomato
pompelmo	- grapefruit
porcini	- highly prized mushroom available in early summer and early autumn
porri	- leeks
pranzo	- most often lunch, but may mean dinner (see cena)
prezzemolo	- parsey
primo	- first course (pasta, rice, soup, etc.)
prosciutto crudo	- salted cured ham
prosciutto cotto	- cooked ham
prugna	- plum (prugna secca - prune)
puree	- mashed potatoes

quaglia	- quail
radicchio	- red chicory
ragú	- meat sauce
ricotta	- fresh, mild soft cheese made from whey
ripieno	- stuffed
riso	- rice
risotto	- refers to rice barely sauteed in oil or butter then cooked very slowly in broth and other flavorings (may vary from onions, leeks, spinach, artichoke and asparagus to shellfish)
rombo	- turbot
rosmarino	- rosemary
rosso	- red (vino rosso - red wine; birra rossa - red beer)
salame	- salami
sale	- salt
salsiccia	- sausage
salvia	- sage
sardine	- sardines
scaloppine	- veal cutlet
scamorza	- firm pear shaped cheese with delicate taste
schiacciata	- a flat bread used for sandwiches or eaten alone salted and dripped with olive oil
secco	- dry
secondo	- second or main course (fish or meat)
sedano	- celery
semifreddo	- gelato with whipped cream folded in
senape	- mustard
seppia	- squid
sogliola	- sole
soprassata	- head cheesesorbetto - fruit sorbet
speck	- ham (marinated, smoked and aged)
spremuta	- freshly squeezed juice: spremuta d'arancia orange juice
spremuta di pompelmo	- grapefruit juice
stracchino	- a very soft, smooth flavorful cheese
stracotto	- beef stewed in tomatoes and red wine
strozzapreti	- ravioli filling without pasta covering
succo di frutta	- fruit juice
sugo	- sauce
surgelato	- frozen
susina	- plum
tacchino	- turkey

tagliatelle	- flat, long egg pasta noodles
tarocco	- a blood orange
tartufo	- truffle
té	- tea
té al latte	- tea with milk
té al limone	- tea with lemon
té freddo	- iced tea, usually already sweetened
tiramisù	- a rich dessert made with mascarpone, liquor, cookies and often, chocolate
tisana	- herbal tea
toast	- grilled ham and cheese sandwich on American style bread
tonno	- tuna
torrone	- nougat candy
torta	- cake
totano	- squid
tovagliolo	- napkin
tramezzino	- sandwich
trippa	- tripe
trota	- trout
uovo	- egg
uva	- grape (uva bianca - green grapes; uva nera - purple grapes)
verdure	- vegetables
verza	- cabbage
vino	- wine
vino da tavola	- table wine
vino della casa	- house wine (often called vino sfuso)
vin santo	- dessert wine
vitella	- heifer, (i.e. young female cow)
vitello	- veal
vongola	- clam
zabaione	- dessert of egg yolks whipped until creamy with sweet wine and sugar
zafferano	- saffron
zampone	- pig shin and foot stuffed with cooked pork sausage
zenzero	- ginger; also hot chili pepper (see: peperoncini)
zucca	- squash
zuppa	- soup

List of pizzerie and Chinese restaurants in Florence.
Addresses found in the general index

Pizzerie

Borgo Antico
La Capanna
La Clara
Il David
Le Follie
Il Gatto e la Volpe
La Luna
Alla Marchigiana
Nuti
Piezzo
Pizzeus
La Scala pizzeria
Lo Spuntino
I Tarocchi
Yellow Bar

Chinese

Fior di Loto
Mandarino
Mister Hang
Nandino
Nuova Cina
Peking
Shangai
Eito (Japanese food)

GENERAL INDEX

ACQUA AL DUE
Via dell'Acqua 2
Tel: 284170
Zone: Piazza della Signoria

ACQUACOTTA
Via dei Pilastri 51/r
Tel: 242907
Zone: Santa Croce

ACQUERELLO
Via Ghibellina 156/r
Tel: 2340554
Zone: Santa Croce

ALFREDO
Via dei Leoni 14
Tel: 294912
Zone: Ponte Vecchio

ALFREDO SULL'ARNO
Via dei Bardi 46/r
Tel: 283808
Zone: Ponte Vecchio

ALESSI
Via di Mezzo 26/r
Tel: 41821
Zone: Santa Croce

ANGIOLINO
Via Santo Spirito 36
Tel: 298976
Zone: Piazza Signoria

ANITA
Via del Parlascio 2
Tel: 218698
Zone: Piazza Signoria

ANTICA CANTINA CAPPONI
Borgo San Frediano 26/r
Tel: 292130
Zone: S.Spirito

ANTICHI CANCELLI
Via Faenza 73
Tel: 218927
North of S. Maria Novella

ANTICO CRESPINO
Largo Fermi 15
Tel: 221158
South Florence (Pog. Imp.)

ANTICO FATTORE
Via Lambertesca 1
Tel: 261215
Zone: Ponte Vecchio

ARMANDO
Borgo Ognissanti 140
Tel: 216219
Zone: Ognissanti

BACCUS
Via Borgo Ognissanti 45/r
Tel: 283714
Zone: Ognissanti

BALDINI
Via Panzani 57/r
Tel: 283331
Zone: Santa Maria Novella

BALDINI TRATTORIA
Via Il Prato 96/r
Tel: 287663
Zone: West of Ognissanti

BALDOVINO
Via San Giuseppe 22
Tel: 241773
Zone: S. Croce

DI BARBANO
Piazza della Indipendenza 3
Tel: 486752
North of Duomo zone

LA BARAONDA
Via Ghibellina 67/r
Tel: 2341171
Zone: Santa Croce

IL BARGELLO
Piazza della Signoria 4/r
Tel: 214071
Zone: Piazza Signoria

BARONE
Via Romano 123/r
Tel: 220585
Zone: Santo Spirito

IL BARROCCIO
Via della Vigna Vecchia 31/r
Tel: 211503
Zone: Santa Croce

BATTISTERO
Via Ricasoli 5/7/r
Tel: 292124
Zone: Duomo

LE BELLE DONNE
Via delle Belle Donne 16/r
Tel: 262609
Zone: Santa Trinità

DA BENVENUTO
Via Mosca 16
Tel: 214833
Zone: Santa Croce

LA BEPPA
Via dell'Erta Canina 6
Tel: 296390
Zone: South of S.Croce

BIBO
Piazza S.Felicità 6-7/r
Tel: 298554
Zone: Ponte Vecchio

IL BIRIBISSO
Via dell'Albero 28/r
Tel: 293180
Zone: S. Maria Novella

BOBOLI
Via Romana 45
Tel: 2336401
Zone: Santo Spirito

BORDINO
Via Stracciatella 9
Tel: 213048
Zone: Ponte Vecchio

BORGHESI
Via de' Calzaiuoli 107
Tel: 211431
Zone: Duomo

BORGO ANTICO
Piazza S.Spirito 6
Tel: 210437
Zone: S.Spirito

DA BRUNO
Via L. Alamanni 29
Tel: 215413
Zone: S.M. Novella

BUCA LAPI
Via Trebbio 3/r
Tel: 213768
Zone: S.Trinità

BUCA MARIO
Piazza degli Ottaviani 16/r
Tel: 214179
Zone: Santa Maria Novella

BUCA DELL'ORAFO
Volta dei Girolami 28
Tel: 213619
Zone: Ponte Vecchio

Buca Poldi
Chiasso degli Armagnati 2/r
Tel: 296578
Zone: Piazza della Signoria

BUCA SAN FIRENZE
Via Condotta 9/r
Tel: 287612
Zone: Piazza Signoria

LA BUSSOLA
Via Porta Rossa 58
Tel: 298013
Zone: Santa Trinita

BUZZINO
Via dei Leoni 8/r
Tel: 298013
Zone: Piazza Signoria

CAFFÈ CONCERTO
Lungarno C.Colombo 7
Tel:677377
Zone: East of the S. Croce

CAMINETTO, IL
Via Studio 34
Tel: 296274
Zone: Duomo

CAMMILLO
Borgo San Jacopo 57/r
Tel: 212427
Zone: Ponte Vecchio

CAMPANE, LE
Borgo la Croce 87
Tel: 678218
Zone: East of S. Croce

CAMPIDOGLIO, AL
Via Campidoglio 8/r
Tel: 287770
Zone: Duomo

CANTINETTA ANTINORI
Piazza Antinori 3
Tel: 292234
Zone: S.Trinita

CANTINONE GALLO NERO
Via Santo Spirito 6/r
Tel: 218898
Zone: S. Spirito

CAPANNA, LA
Via Cavour 112
Tel: 210095
Zone: Duomo

La Capannina Di Sante
Ponte da Verrazzano/Piazza Ravenna
Tel: 688345
2.500 mt. east of Ponte Vecchio

La Carabaccia
Via Palazzuolo 190
Tel: 214782
Zone: Ognissanti

Del Carmine
Piazza del Crmine 18
Tel: 218601
Zone: Santo Spirito

Casa Del Vin Santo
Via Porta Rossa 25/27/r
Tel: 216995
Zone: Piazza Signoria

Cavallino
Piazza della Signoria
Tel: 215818
Zone: Piazza Signoria

Cave Di Maiano
Via delle Cave 16 Maiano
Tel: 59133
(Fiesole) 5Km north of city

Celestino
Piazza Santa Felicità 4
Tel: 296574
Zone: Ponte Vecchio

Centanni
Via Centanni 7
Bagno a Ripoli
Tel: 630122

Cibreo
Via de'Macci 118
Tel: 2341100
Zone: Santa Croce

Cinque Amici
Via dei Cimatori 30
Tel: 296672
Zone: Piazza Signoria

Clara
Borgo Santa Croce 59
Tel: 667083
Zone: S. Croce

Coco Lezzone
Via Parioncino 26
Tel: 287178
Zone: S.Trinita

Coccodrillo, Il
Via della Scala 5
Tel: 283622
Zone: Ognissanti

Conca D'Oro, La
Piazza della Indipendenza 3
Tel: 486752
North of Duomo zone

Corona
Via Nazionale 90
Tel: 294256
Zone: Santa Maria Novella

Corsini
Lungarno Corsini 4
Tel: 217706
Zone: S.Trinita

DA COSIMO
Via dell'Oriuolo 16
Tel: 2480410
Zone: Duomo

CROCE AL TREBBIO
Via delle Belle Donne 49
Tel: 287O89
Zone: Santa Maria Novella

CUSCUSSU
Via L. C. Farini 2/r
Tel: 241890
Zone: Santa Croce

DANNY ROCK
Via Pandolfini 13
Tel: 2340307
Zone: Santa Croce

DA NOI
Via Fiesolana 40/r
Tel: 242917
Zone: Santa Croce

DAVID
Piazza della Signoria
Tel: 292188
Zone: Piazza Signoria

DILADDARNO
Via Serragli 108/r
Tel: 225001
Zone: Santo Spirito

DINO
Via Finiguerra 8/r
Tel: 287088
Zone: Santa Croce

DINO
Via Ghibellina 51/r
Tel: 241452
Zone: Santa Croce

DON CHISCIOTTE
Via Ridolfi 4
Tel: 475430
North of Duomo zone

DONEY
Piazza Strozzi 18
Tel: 298206/218556
Zone: Santa Trinita

I DUE "G"
Via V.B. Cennini 6/r
Tel: 218623
Zone: Santa Maria Novella

EDO
Via Guelfa 81/r
Tel: 218865
North of S. Maria Novella

DA EDY
Piazza Savonarola 9/r
Tel: 588886
Zone: North of Duomo

EITO (JAPANESE)
Via dei Neri 72
Tel: 210940
Zone: Piazza Signoria

ENOTECA PINCHIORRI
Via Ghibellina 87
Tel: 242777
Zone: S. Croce

ENZO & PIERO
Via Faenza 105
Tel: 214901
Zone: Santa Maria Novella

IL FAGIANO
Via dei Neri 57/r
Tel: 287876
Zone: Santa Croce

DEL FAGIOLI
Corso dei Tintori 47/r
Tel: 2480170
Zone: Santa Croce

FALTERONA
Via Zannoni 10
Tel: 216112
Zone: S. Maria Novella

FIOR DI LOTO
Via dei Servi 35/r
Tel: 2398235
Zone: Duomo

LE FOLLIE
Lungarno Tempio 52
Tel: 2343693
Zone: East of S. Croce

LE FONTICINE
Via Nazionale 9/r
Tel: 82106
Zone: S. Maria Novella

FORTUNATO
Via Palazzuolo 31
Tel: 218846
Zone: Ognissanti

I'FRANCESCANO
Via S.Giuseppe 26
Tel: 241605
Zone: S. Croce

GABRIELLO
Via Condotta 54
Tel: 212098
Zone: Piazza Signoria

LA GALLERIA
Via de' Guicciardini 48
Tel: 218545
Zone: Ponte Vecchio

GANINO OSTERIA
Piazza Cimatori 4
Tel: 214125
Zone: Piazza Signoria

GARGA
Via Moro 46/R
TEL: 298898
Zone: Santa Maria Novella

IL GATTO E LA VOLPE
Via Gibellina 151
Tel: 2432634
Zone: S. Croce

GAUGUIN
Via degli Alfani 24/r
Tel: 2340616
Zone: Duomo

DI GENNARO
Via de' Castellani 4
Tel: 218822
Zone: Piazza Signoria

GERSHWIN
Via Alfani 26/r
Tel: 2341606
Zone: Duomo

GHIBELLINI, I
Piazza S.Pier Maggiore 8
Tel: 214424
Zone: S. Croce

GIANNINO IN SAN LORENZO
Borgo San Lorenzo 35
Tel: 212206
Zone: Duomo

DA GIGI
Via Del Gigi 14/r
Tel: 218563
Zone: S. Maria Novella

GIGLIO ROSSO
Via de' Panzani 35/r
Tel: 211795
Zone: S. Maria Novella

I GOLOSI
Via Pandolfini 13
Tel: 2340307
Zone: S. Croce

GOURMET
Via Il Prato 68
Tel: 294766
Zone: Ognissanti

GRAZIELLA
Via delle Cave, Maiano
Tel: 599963
5 km north of Florence

GREPPIA
Lungarno Ferrucci 4
Tel: 6812341
South of S. Croce

GRIGLIA, LA
Piazza della Stazione 42
Tel: 2398141
Zone: S. Maria Novella

GROTTA GUELFA
Via Pellicceria 5
Tel: 210042
Zone: Piazza Signoria

GUSCIO
Via dell'Orto 49/r
Tel: 224421
Zone: Santo Spirito

HARRY'S BAR
Lungarno Vespucci 22
Tel: 2936700
Zone: Ognissanti

I CHE C'È C'È
Via de' Magalotti 11
Tel: 262867
Zone: Piazza Signoria

LAMPARA
Via Nazionale 36
Tel: 215164
Zone: S. Maria Novella

LATINI
Via Palchetti 6
Tel: 210976
Zone: Santa Trinita

LEO IN SANTA CROCE
Via Torta 7
Tel: 210829
Zone: S. Croce

LA LOGGIA
Piazzale Michelangelo 1
Tel: 287032
South of S. Croce

LORENZACCIO
Via B. Rucellai 1
Tel: 217100
Just west of S. Maria Novella

AL LUME DI CANDELA
Via delle Terme 23/r
Tel: 294566
Zone: Ponte Vecchio

MACELLERIA
Via San Zanobi 97/r
Tel: 486244
North of Duomo zone

MAMMA GINA
Borgo San Jacopo 37
Tel: 296009
Zone: Piazza Signoria

MANDARINO
Via Condotta 17
Tel: 296130
Zone: Piazza Signoria

MARCHIGIANA
Via Corso 60
Tel: 214961
Zone: Duomo

LA MAREMMA
Via G.Verdi 16
Tel: 244615
Zone: S. Croce

LA MAREMMANA
Via dei Macci 77/r
Tel: 241226
Zone: S. Croce

MARINO
Via della Canonica 1
Tel: 210285
Zone: Duomo

MARIO
Via Rosina 2
Tel: 218550
Zone: S. Maria Novella

MARIONE
Via della Spada 27/r
Tel: 214756
Zone: Santa Trinita

MARTINICCA
Via Del Sole 27
Tel: 2128928
Zone: S. Maria Novella

MAXIMILLIAN
Via degli Alfani 10
Tel: 2478080
Zone: Duomo

MISTER HANG
Via Ghibellina 134
Tel: 2344810
Zone: S. Croce

MONKEY BUSINESS
Chiasso dei Baroncelli
Tel: 288219
Zone: Piazza Signoria

MONNALISA
Via Faenza 4
Tel: 210298
Zone: S. Maria Novella

MONTECATINI
Via dei Leoni 6
Tel: 284863
Zone: Piazza Signoria

LE MOSSACCE
Via del Proconsolo 55
Tel: 294361
Zone: Duomo

MURATE
Via Ghibellina 52/r
Tel: 240618
Zone: S. Croce

NANCHINO
Via dei Cerchi 40
Tel: 213024
Zone: Piazza Signoria

NANDINA
Borgo SS. Apostoli 64/r
Tel: 213024
Zone: Santa Trinita

NANNONI
Piazza Duomo 27
Tel: 216678
Zone: Duomo

NATALE
Lungarno Acciaioli 80
Tel: 213968
Zone: Ponte Vecchio

NATALINO
Borgo Albizi 17
Tel: 263404
Zone: S. Croce

NELLA
Via delle Terme 19/r
Tel: 218924
Zone: Ponte Vecchio

NELLO
Borgo Pinti 56/r
Tel: 2478410
North of S. Croce

NELLO
Borgo Tegolaio 21/r
Tel: 218511
Zone: Santo Spirito

NUOVA CAMPANA
Borgo San Lorenzo 24/r
Tel: 211326
Zone: Duomo

NUOVA CINA
Piazza S. Maria Novella 9
Tel: 215387
Zone: S. Maria Novella

NUTI
Borgo San Lorenzo 24
Tel: 210145
Zone: Duomo

OMERO
Via del Pian dei Giullari 11
Tel: 220053
2 Km south of Florence

ORCAGNA
Piazza della Signoria 1
Tel: 292188
Zone: Piazza Signoria

ORESTE
Piazza Santo Spirito 16
Tel: 262383
Zone: Santo Spirito

OSTERIA NUMERO UNO
Via del Moro 18
Tel: 284897/294318
Zone: S. Maria Novella

OSTERIA CINGHIALE BIANCO
Borgo San Jacopo 43
Tel: 215706
Zone: Ponte Vecchio

OTELLO
Via degli Oricellari 36
Tel: 215819
Zone: S. Maria Novella

OTTORINO
Via delle Oche 20
Tel: 218747
Zone: Duomo

PAIOLO
Via del Corso 42/r
Tel: 215019
Zone: Duomo

PALLOTINO
Via Isola delle Stinche 1/r
Tel: 289573
Zone: S. Croce

PAOLI
Via dei Tavolini 12
Tel: 216215
Zone: Piazza Signoria

PERBACCO
Borgo Tegolaio 21/r
Tel: 218511
Zone: Santo Spirito

PEKING
Via del Melarancio 21
Tel: 282922
Zone: S. Maria Novella

PENNELLO
Via D. Alighieri 4
Tel: 294848
Zone: Duomo

PEPE VERDE
Piazza Mercato Centrale 17
Tel: 283906
Zone: Duomo

PENTOLA D'ORO
Via Mezzo 26
Tel: 241808
Zone: S. Croce

PEPOLINO
Via Ferrucci 16
Tel: 608905
East of S. Croce

PIEZZO
Via dei Neri 40
Tel: 217718
Zone: S. Croce

PINOCCHIO
Via della Scala 28
Tel: 218418
Zone: S. Maria Novella

PIZZEUS
Viale Gramsci 9/11 r
Tel: 672980
Zone: North east of S. Croce

POSTA
Via Pellicceria 28/r
Tel: 212701
Zone: Piazza Signoria

IL PROFETA
Borgo Ognissanti 93
Tel: 212265
Zone: Ognissanti

PRO-POLIS 80
Borgo Pinti 10/r
Tel: 2480470
Zone: S. Croce

QUATTRO LEONI
Via Vellutini 1/r
Tel: 218562
Zone: Ponte Vecchio

QUATTRO STAGIONI
Via Maggio 61
Tel: 218906
Zone: S. Spirito

QUINTO
Piazza dei Peruzzi 5
Tel: 213323
Zone: S. Croce

RADDI
Via dell'Ardiglione 47/r
Tel: 211072
Zone: Santo Spirito

Rampe
Viale G. Poggi 1
Tel: 6811891
Zone: south of S. Croce

ROSE'S CAFE
Via del Parione 26
Tel: 287090
Zone: S. Trinita

RUCOLA
Via del Leone 50/r
Tel: 224002
South west of Santo Spirito

SABATINI
Via Panzani 41
Tel: 211559
Zone: S. Maria Novella

SAGRESTIA
Via de'Giucciardini 27
Tel: 210003
Zone: Ponte Vecchio

SAN AGOSTINO
Via San Agostino 23
Tel: 210208
Zone: Santo Spirito

SASSO DI DANTE
Piazza delle Pallottole 6
Tel: 282113
Zone: Duomo

SCALA PIZZERA
Borgo La Croce 59
Tel: 2480783
Zone: S. Croce

SCOGLIO 90
Via dei Lavatoi 13/r
Tel: 2344880
Zone: S. Croce

SERRAGLI
Via de' Serragli 108
Tel: 225001
Zone: Santo Spirito

SHANGAI
Piazza della Libertà 32
Tel: 583596
North of Duomo

SILIO, DA
Via Guelfa 90/r
Tel: 475291
Zone: North of S.M. Novella

SILVIO
Via del Parione 74
Tel: 214005
Zone: Santo Trinita

SORELLE
Via di San Niccolo 30
Tel: 284422
East of S. Croce zone

SOSTANZA
Via del Porcellana 25/r
Tel: 212691
Zone: Ognissanti

SPADA
Via del Moro 66/r
Tel: 218757
Zone: S. Maria Novella

SPUNTINO
Via del Canto de' Nelli 14
Tel: 210920
Zone: Duomo

STRETTOIO
Via Serpiolle 7
Tel: 403044
Zone: 5Km north of city

TAROCCHI
Via de' Renai 14/r
Tel: 2343912
South of S. Croce

TAVERNA DEL BRONZINO
Via delle Ruote 25/r
Tel: 495220
North of S. Maria Novella

TEATRO
Via degli Alfani 47
Tel: 2479327
Zone: Duomo

TIRABUSCIO
Via dei Benci 34
Tel: 2476225
Zone: S. Croce

Tito
Via San Gallo 112
Tel: 472475
North of Duomo zone

Toto
Borgo SS Apostoli 6/r
Tel: 212096
Zone: Ponte Vecchio

Toula
Via delle Terme 51/r
Tel: 287643
Zone: Santa Trinita

Trattoria Casalinga
Via del Michelozzi, 9 red
Tel: 218624
Zone: Santo Spirito

Tredici Gobbi
Via del Porcellana 9
Tel: 298769
Zone: Ognissanti

Vecchia Bettola
Viale L. Ariosto 34
Tel: 224158
Piazza Tasso (S. Spirito)

Vecchia Cucina
Viale Amicis 1
Tel: 660143
Zone: Near Stadium

Vecchia Firenze
Borgo degli Albizi 18
Tel: 294163
Zone: S. Croce

Yellow Bar
Via del Proconsolo 39
Tel: 211766
Zone: Duomo

La Vie en Rose
Borgo Allegri 68r
Tel: 245860
Zone: S. Croce

Zi Rosa
Via de' Fossi 12/r
Tel: 287062
Zone: S. Maria Novella

Zà Zà
Piaz. Mercato Centrale 26/r
Tel: 215411
Zone: Duomo

Zodiaco
Via delle Casine 2
Tel: 2340984
Zone: S. Croce